MW00630370

THE WICKMAN FORMULA

THE WICKMAN FORMULA

Seven Steps to Achieving Your Full Potential

Floyd Wickman

Library of Congress Cataloging in Publication Data

ISBN 0–939975–06–8

Published by Executive Press
806 Westchester Drive
High Point, NC 27262

Printed in the United States of America.

Dedication

This book is dedicated to my father whom I've
always loved
and now understand
was the best man he could be.

Acknowledgements

I figure there were thousands of people who positively affected my life. But I can think specifically of 26 people who influenced me and helped me reach my full potential. In chronological order, I want to thank: Gert and Floyd, Mr. Holt, Gino Tiracchia, Rich Behring, "H.B.," Jim Bell and Matt Kamer, Og Mandino, Bob Mohr, Zig Ziglar, Linda, my wife, my sons, Floyd, Gino and David, Bill McCullen, Steven Linn, Mark Murray, Marty Reuter, Art Fettig, Bill Gove, Mike F., Debbie Williams, Jim Murray and Ed Escobar, and Elliot Wagenheim.

Contents

Introduction

Floyd Wickman's hobby is woodworking, which is appropriate. Woodworking requires that you start with a piece of raw lumber, cut away what you don't need, then smooth off the rough edges to get some beautiful results. Floyd's life started out like a piece of raw wood with a lot of rough edges in need of smoothing off. From that original timber, something nice has emerged—thanks to a great deal of hard work and some lessons learned along the way. This book will tell how that happened, and how the lessons learned by one man who once seemed trapped in mediocrity can help you to achieve greatness in whatever you pursue.

This book is written by Floyd Wickman about Floyd Wickman, but you'll find the author constantly referring to himself in the third person. That's because he periodically calls upon his double—call him Floyd II—to do the narrating. Floyd II enables the real Floyd to step back for a little perspective; to look at himself a little more objectively. This device also saves wear and tear on the "I" key of the word processor. Floyd is not comfortable reading books by authors who get hung up on the pronoun "I." It always seems to him that such authors are self-centered, focusing attention on themselves. He wants this book to be focused as much as possible on the content and not on the author. When Floyd II is writing, the material will appear in italics, as in the case of this introduction.

This book will also focus on Floyd Wickman's experiences. They are the experiences of a man who at one point seemed to be destined for a life as a paycheck slave—working day and night just to put food on the table and a roof over the head of his family. Yet, after many years of failing, Floyd found himself and found the formula for success. His "rags-to-riches" story, from a ninth grade dropout to an internationally known teacher of success principles, is designed to inspire and help you achieve your full potential.

The early Floyd Wickman committed his share of mischief with the gang of kids he hung out with on the east side of Detroit. He spent close to a decade as an enlisted man in the Navy, going nowhere in particular except wherever his ship bore him. He spent one hard year trying to make it in real estate, not knowing the formula that could unlock the door to greatness.

And then something happened. Floyd Wickman became aware that he could become a success. This awareness opened the door. He began doing the things that enabled him to become a successful real estate salesman. It wasn't long before his production put him in the top 0.1% of all the real estate agents in North America. Next he became sales manager for his real estate company. Soon he was setting company sales records that have not been touched since. After that, he decided to become a sales trainer. He began by training individuals in a real estate office and eventually became national training director for one of the country's largest real estate franchise organizations.

One day, sitting in an audience of 2,300 people, Floyd heard a speaker issue a call to greatness. He decided, on the spot, to be a professional speaker. Eleven years later, he had spoken to more than 2,000 audiences in 50 states, eight Canadian provinces and several other countries. He had earned the National Speakers Association's Council of Peers Award of Excellence—the Oscar of the speaking profession.

Now he is the CEO of a multimillion dollar corporation, has dozens of trainers from coast to coast on his staff and as of this writing is a finalist for 1991 Entrepreneur of the Year. The Floyd Wickman Course, a sales and management training program, is being taught to thousands of enrollees each month. Tens of thousands of people have seen their careers take off after completing this course.

Introduction

Several million Floyd Wickman audio cassettes are being used daily in the sales and management industry.

The young lad who started out running with a pack of kids on Detroit's east side is now a respected business executive who practices his corporate motto: "We get by giving." What's more, he is a stable family man with a beautiful wife and three successful sons.

Floyd Wickman's road to success began in a real estate office and took him through sales management, sales training and public speaking. But the principles that served him can also serve you, no matter what calling you pursue. This book represents his effort to help others to accomplish their goals as he has accomplished his.

Do you feel trapped at an unsatisfactory point in your life? Welcome to the club; Floyd has been there. Do you consider yourself a hard worker with nothing to show for your effort? Floyd has been there too. Does your poor self-image restrict you from desiring more in life? He's been there too. Do you feel you lack what it takes to succeed? So did he. But he found a way out of these traps, and he's confident that you can spring yourself free by following the same formula. You can go from mediocrity to greatness the same way Floyd did.

Don't be scared off by the word "greatness." To achieve "greatness" in your life, you don't have to have the accomplishments of a George Washington or Thomas Edison or Henry Ford. Floyd uses the word to mean achieving your full potential.

Let the word "greatness" mean all the good things you want from life. Greatness could be one thing for you, another thing for your neighbor, another thing for Floyd Wickman. It could be taking control of your life. It could be a salesperson making the Million-Dollar Sales Club. It could be being free and clear of debt. It could be being president of the United States, an alderman in your home town, or the top performer in your industry. Decide upon your own definition of greatness and aim for it. Don't be afraid of aiming too high. Someone once said that it's better to aim for a star and hit an eagle than it is to aim for an eagle and hit a rock.

In this book, Floyd gives you The Wickman Formula—a tested and proven method for achieving all the good things you want in life. It consists of **Seven Steps.** *Follow these steps and you'll achieve your full potential.*

Don't be discouraged by the thought that you don't have the stuff of greatness. Everybody possesses the potential for greatness. That doesn't mean that you can be great at everything. If your aptitude lies in the area of space science, you're probably not going to make it as a rock star. But you've got great potential as a space scientist. If you're an introverted watchmaker, you'll have a hard time making it as a national politician. But you may be the person who gives the world the next great advance in timekeeping—or in some other area that fascinates you.

You'll probably find your greatest success in the area that holds the strongest interest for you.

Whatever your natural inclination is, you can follow it all the way from mediocrity to "greatness." Before Floyd embarked on the steps to achieving his full potential, he had to learn four basic lessons. *It took him many years to absorb them. It won't take you as long if you learn the lessons through Floyd Wickman's experiences. Those lessons will be outlined in Part One of this book. They are:*

- ☐ **(Lesson 1)** ***Early choices don't have to bind you for life.***
- ☐ **(Lesson 2)** ***You can't rise to greatness on a bad self-image.***
- ☐ **(Lesson 3)** ***If you don't know what you want, mediocrity is what you'll get.***
- ☐ **(Lesson 4)** ***Greatness won't find you; you have to go after it.***

After you've learned these lessons, you're ready to start taking the ***Seven Steps to Achieving Your Full Potential.*** *They are;*

- ☐ **(Step 1)** ***Wake up to your capacity for greatness.***
- ☐ **(Step 2)** ***Establish your goals—great ones and small ones.***
- ☐ **(Step 3)** ***Make a commitment.***
- ☐ **(Step 4)** ***Work hard and work smart.***
- ☐ **(Step 5)** ***Give unselfishly in order to get.***
- ☐ **(Step 6)** ***Give yourself a raise.***
- ☐ **(Step 7)** ***Practice the "Dance of Greatness."***

The lessons and the **Seven Steps** *will become more meaningful as we elaborate on them. But the important thing to remember is this: You don't have to be stuck in mediocrity. You don't have to settle for less than your full potential.*

These lessons are not "how-to's." We'll cover those later. The lessons are those discoveries that tell you that you are ready to start taking the necessary steps toward achieving your full potential. They are the "thought-provokers" that tell you it's okay to work toward greatness. Let me put it another way: The **Seven Steps** *won't work if you don't know the lessons. And knowing the lessons without following the* **Seven Steps** *will lead to nowhere. They are just to get you ready. There is an old saying: When the student is ready, the teacher appears.*

A PROVEN FORMULA

A group of journalists once were questioning an ex-farmer who had made his way to the governor's mansion in his native state. After his term as governor, he had seemed destined to retire to the farm and to historical obscurity. But he glimpsed other possibilities.

As governor of his state, he told the journalists, he saw a number of illustrious national leaders come and go as guests in the governor's mansion. Some of them were considered presidential timber. He had an opportunity to talk with them, one on one. Gradually, it dawned upon him that they were no smarter than he.

So he decided to make his own bid for the presidency. He went to a Midwestern state where no one had ever heard of him before, and he began extending his hand and introducing himself.

"Hi," he would say in his high-pitched Southern drawl. "I'm Jimmy Carter." The people of Iowa loved him, and his victory in the Democratic caucuses gave him the boost he needed to launch his successful drive toward the presidency.

Jimmy Carter would never have made it to the White House without the recognition that he had it in him to be something more than a peanut farmer.

We use Jimmy because his rise from farmer to president best exemplifies the theme of this book. We could have used Harry; we could have used Abe; we could have used Andy. Or we could have used Jimmy's immediate predecessor, Jerry—the guy who told the American people, "I'm a Ford, not a Lincoln."

Jimmy Carter had learned the same lessons Floyd eventually learned, and he followed the same process toward the presidency. So did Abe, so did Jerry, so did Harry.

So did a lot of other people who never made it to the White House. One of them was Danielle Kennedy, a California woman who has achieved greatness as a speaker in the real estate industry.

At one point in her life, Danielle had five small children and was pregnant with a sixth. She had a whole lifetime of misfortunes to use as an excuse for mediocrity. But she decided to aim for greatness. Greatness, by her definition, was becoming the top woman real estate salesperson and real estate speaker in the country. She has achieved that greatness, and you can bet, if you asked her, that she would tell you she rose to her current level by being aware of these same four lessons and following the same seven-step process.

Tom Monaghan is another ordinary person who learned the lessons Floyd learned. He started out in the pizza business in

Ypsilanti, Michigan, with a $75 down payment, a lot of hope and not much else. His place didn't have enough room for more than four customers, so he decided to make his money by delivering pizzas, which was a pretty lofty ambition for a man who couldn't afford a telephone at the outset. But Tom Monaghan built that small business into the multibillion-dollar Domino's Pizza chain, which now stretches from coast to coast. If you and he could analyze it, you'd see that he achieved that success for the same reason: the lessons and the steps.

All of these people, and countless others, rose above a crowd of contemporaries because they could see the potential for greatness that lay beyond their ordinary circumstances. They too followed this formula.

Your goal may not be the White House. But whatever goal you choose, you can reach it, and achieve your full potential, by heeding the four lessons in this book, then embarking on the **Seven Steps.**

IT WORKED FOR AN ORDINARY GUY

It's a simple process, but it works. It worked for an uneducated, destined-to-failure guy by the name of Floyd Wickman, and it has worked for many others.

Remember: Floyd's not claiming to be a hero or a genius. He's just an ordinary guy who looked up one day, saw a world of possibilities, and decided to go after them. Those possibilities are out there for you, too. Floyd hopes this book will help you see them and achieve them. And if, as you work toward your goals, you see through your mind's eye a guy who's cheering you on like a boxing fan at ringside, that will be Floyd Wickman. Go to it.

Part One

FOUR EARLY LESSONS

Lesson One

Early Choices Don't Have to Bind You For Life

Okay, so you made a lot of bum decisions early in life, and they've come back to haunt you. Don't let them. Your early choices don't have to doom you to mediocrity for the rest of your life. My life began turning around at the age of 26 when I became aware of that fact. You can make the same kind of turnaround.

Don't be turned off by a lot of negative sayings you've heard all your life.

"I am what I am, and that's what I am," said Popeye the sailor.

"You've made your bed, and now you've got to lie in it," said countless parents to sons and daughters who had made foolish decisions.

If you want to spend your life making excuses for failure, believe what Popeye and countless parents have said. Throw up your hands, say "You can't teach an old dog new tricks," then slink off with your tail between your legs. If you believe all that negative stuff, you'll find that the negative stuff is true.

But if you believe positive things, you'll find that they can prove to be just as true. If you want to spend your life moving firmly toward success, believe Floyd Wickman: You don't have to be a prisoner of your early decisions in life.

Too many people have been trapped by the "I-can't-change" attitude. They say: "Hey, I've been a rock all my life. Don't start chipping and sanding and polishing to try to make me into a diamond. I'll never be anything but a rock."

To prepare yourself for success, you've got to turn that attitude around.

"I was what I was. I will be what I want to be. And right now, I want to be successful and I'm going to go for greatness." If you take that attitude, you're on your way to achieving greatness.

You need to understand that the past is the past. Whatever choices you made in the past belong in the past. The future is out there to be won, and you don't win it by sitting around moping over the past.

It took me years to discover that I was using my past as an anchor toward my future. I was simply trapped in the past and didn't have to be. I learned that there is nothing special about successful people; it's what they do, not who they are that counts.

A STORY OF BAD CHOICES

Believe me, when it comes to bad choices, I made some lulus. But when I decided to go for greatness, I left those choices in the past. I refused to be bound by them. I chose to control the future by the new choices I would make.

Let me tell you about some of those choices.

CATS AND SQUARES

On the east side of Detroit in the middle '50s, you were either a cat or a square. A kid had to make a choice, and it was no light decision. It determined who you were and where you were going.

Floyd chose to become a cat. If you were to travel back in time to his old neighborhood in the fall of 1954, you'd see him on a street corner with Buster, Bill, Dale and Eric. See that kid with the slicked-back hair wearing the leather jacket with "El Duches" written across the back? That's Floyd Wickman, age 13.

What are they doing?

What cats always do on a fall evening in Detroit. It's also what they always do in winter and summer and spring. Hanging around.

Maybe they look like they're goofing off, but in Floyd's circle of friends, this is serious business. They're learning how to walk, talk and stare. They're practicing for their roles in life. They know that unless they get those moves and looks down perfectly, they're going to end up as squares, which is a fate worse than zits.

Cat or square. In Detroit in 1954, these are your options. In the world of the 1990s, kids will have lots of options. They'll be able to select from a menu of labels. Punch a computer key and pull them up on the screen: jock or preppie, liberal or conservative, gay or straight, yuppie or working stiff, stockbroker or burger-flipper. But on the east side of Detroit in the 1950s, you're either a cat or a square, and the rest don't count.

HOW TO TELL THE DIFFERENCE

It's easy to tell a square from a cat. Squares are the guys who get good grades in school. They never skip. The school counselors don't even know their names, because they never see them. You see the counselor when you screw up, right? Squares don't screw up. They focus their attention on learning to please their teachers and parents, just as cats focus their attention on learning to walk and talk and stare. Counselors are not there to help kids; they're there to punish. They ought to be called probation officers. Squares don't need punishing. They already fit smoothly into their square holes and there's no need to chisel off any rough edges.

It's the cats who need punishing. They're nothing ***but*** *rough edges, and they show them off the way a Marine shows off the medals he won at the Chosen Reservoir.*

Cats never get good grades in school. They can't; it just isn't cool. Getting good grades would mean surrendering all claims to cathood. It would automatically make you a square and stigmatize you forever.

You can tell cats by the way they look: hair plastered back with Dixie Peach pomade, or pulled to the front into the waterfall. Black leather jackets with the names of street gangs on the backs.

But it's the walk that validates your status. You can fake the jacket and the hair, but not the walk. If a guy looks like a cat but walks straight, you know immediately that he's a square.

That's why a cat spends so much time on his walk. He could be spending time learning to do algebra, learning to communicate in standard English, learning about chemistry and physics and all the other things that might boost him toward greatness when it comes time to enter the real world.

But to concentrate on those things would be to choose the priorities of a square. And no cat wants to do anything that might lead anybody to suspect him of being square. So instead of hitting the books, he hits the sidewalk to perfect his walk.

That calls for practice, practice, practice: Take a long step forward with your left foot while you simultaneously roll your right shoulder. Then you sort of drag your right foot up to where it's supposed to be, remembering to keep your arms low and your hands cupped to the back. If you can do that, no matter how you dress, people will take you for a cat.

THE RULES FOR BEING A CAT

There were rules a guy had to follow if he wanted to be a cat in the '50s. Here are some of them:

- ❑ *Never smile, especially when girls are around. Smiling doesn't fit the cat image. Keep a squint-eyed stare, with the head bobbing up and down. Now you're swinging.*
- ❑ *You have to smoke. How can you look cool without a cigarette in your mouth and a pack in your jacket pocket?*
- ❑ *You must keep doing things against society so that you will get caught by the cops. Remember, only squares never get into trouble.*
- ❑ *Never take lip from anybody, no matter how big he may be. (I violated that rule on occasion; sometimes survival takes precedence over being a cat.)*
- ❑ *It's okay to work part-time, so long as you complain about it in front of everyone.*

CHOICES THAT LEAD NOWHERE

Such were the choices made by the cool cats of Detroit in the middle '50s. Such were the choices of Floyd Wickman, son of a milkman, lover of girls and good times, quintessential cat. In retrospect, Floyd realizes that choosing to be a cat was admitting to the self-image of a loser. Some people make those early choices and honestly believe that they must always be what they are—a rock.

Let me tell you straight out what those choices get you in the serious business of life: ZILCH. Floyd Wickman knows from sad experience that greatness doesn't come out of a jar of Dixie Peach pomade; that it doesn't come in a jacket emblazoned with the name of some street gang; and that you don't walk into it by emulating the gait of a street-wise hipster.

Yet those were his choices in the middle 50s, when he was moving toward adulthood. He branded himself a loser. Had he stuck by them, he would still be living from paycheck to paycheck, wallowing in mediocrity and wondering how he was going to pay the next light bill.

DECIDE ON GREATNESS

Success came because I made a new decision that repealed all those earlier decisions. The decision I made was to reach for greatness. It was a decision reached only after I had become aware of the possibilities open to me. I looked up and saw a world of opportunity. I looked inward and found the motivation to seize the opportunity. I learned what was required to achieve success, and was elated to learn that I didn't have to be a Napoleon or a Rockefeller to find greatness. I didn't have to be a Ford, much less a Lincoln. I could succeed just by being a Floyd Wickman. And you can succeed just by being yourself. You don't have to change who you are; just accept who you are and accept the fact that the past is just that—the past.

THE SLOW DANCE OF SUCCESS

That doesn't mean that success will come automatically, without disappointment or setback, once you've made the decision to achieve. In Floyd's experience, nearly every success has been preceded by failure. His route to success has been like a slow dance: two steps backward, three steps forward. But you have to let those two backward steps set the stage for the three steps forward.

So Floyd Wickman, the kid from the east side of Detroit, swapped the cool saunter of the cat for the ***Seven Steps to Achieving Your Full Potential.*** *It took him a while to learn the lessons that prepare you for the* ***Seven Steps.*** *He did the usual things kids did on the streets of Detroit: went to parties, chased girls, went joy-riding—in general, goofed off. He even spent a brief time in juvenile detention with a couple of pals. They "borrowed" cars without asking the owners' permission.*

Had Floyd realized earlier that the choices of the past don't bind you for the future, he would have applied himself in school as he later applied himself in business. He could have skipped a lot of unproductive years. But that would have meant, in his mind, becoming a square, and he chose to stay a cat.

Had he realized that the choice he made then became irrelevant once he entered the Navy, he might have risen through the enlisted ranks and—who knows—eventually gone to school and become an officer. But his ambitions didn't lie in that direction.

MEDIOCRITY OR GREATNESS: IT'S YOUR CHOICE

Maybe your attitude has been similar to mine. Maybe you still see yourself as a cat. If that's what you want to do with your life, it's your choice. But walking and talking and staring like a cat won't put bread on your table, won't buy you that vacation home at the beach, and won't pay for a sharp set of wheels.

The good news is that you don't have to be a cat all your life. There's more good news: Being successful doesn't mean leading a dull life. When you go for greatness, it's an exciting experience. And with greatness in your chosen pursuit comes the ability to acquire the things you like and to do the things you enjoy.

So let the first lesson I learned in life be an important lesson in your life: If you want the better things, you have to realize that the early choices do not have to bind you for life. Forget about what you were and what you are. Focus on what you can be. Follow me through the succeeding chapters, and you'll learn to make the choices that lead to greatness.

List the most important points you have gained from the preceding Lesson:

Lesson Two

You Can't Rise to Greatness On a Bad Self-Image

If you're going to rise to greatness, you've got to believe in yourself. That's the second lesson I've learned in life.

If you see yourself as a failure, you're going to fail. If you see yourself as an achiever, you're going to succeed. We're going to look at some of the things that may cause you to feel like a failure, then look for ways to remove those factors. When you teach yourself to think and feel like a winner, you're going to be on your way to greatness.

For some people, it's easy. They seem to be born with self-confidence. They know as soon as the obstetrician spanks the breath into them that the world is their oyster and everywhere they look they're going to find pearls.

IMAGE ISN'T FACE AND FORM

For some of us, though, self-confidence is hard to come by. If you're a man, maybe it's because you don't have the physique of Arnold Schwarzenegger or the charm of Robert Redford. If you're a woman, you may feel that you don't have the face or the figure or the personality to succeed.

These are all superficial things and they're important only if you make them important. Abe Lincoln was an ugly duckling who never turned into a swan. Nobody ever accused Albert Einstein of being handsome. Do you think anybody would ever cast Lee Iacocca as James Bond? And if you're looking on the feminine side, Eleanor Roosevelt, Golda Meir, Margaret Mead, Gertrude Stein, Indira Gandhi and Dr. Ruth each would have bombed if she had based her self-esteem solely on her physical appearance.

So don't get down on yourself just because you don't have the looks of a matinee idol or a magazine cover girl. Find out how to groom yourself to look your best. Tell yourself that you look great and guess what? You'll look great.

HOME ENVIRONMENT

Some of us have to overcome more than so-so looks, though. Some people grow up in supportive home environments that seem to program them for success. Others grow up in surroundings that, in one way or another, discourage them from developing self-esteem.

If you grew up in such an environment, that's no reason to throw up your hands and quit. The potential for greatness is within you no matter what kind of environment you grew up in. All you have to do is recognize it and see yourself for what you are: a person with enormous potential waiting to be developed. Forget the way things were. Start planning for things the way you want them to be.

THE IMAGE OF A SCREW-UP

Floyd Wickman knows whereof he speaks. He wasn't born with a silver spoon in his mouth, and he didn't have a family of cheerleaders rallying around him and shouting, "Go Floyd, Go!"

Though he did not have a deprived childhood from the standpoint of material things, he did miss out on the warmth and encouragement that build self-esteem in children. Floyd's dad was a milkman, which meant he earned enough to support a family, although he didn't always handle his money wisely. He was a perfectionist in many ways, though, which can be tough on the self-esteem of a less-than-perfect youngster.

So Floyd grew up thinking of himself as a screw-up. Maybe it's because he seems to have screwed up just about everything he tried the first time around. He probably took a wrong turn coming out of the womb, which may be the reason his mom thought she had appendicitis instead of a pregnancy. Somehow, little Floyd got his bearings, though, located the birth canal and squirmed his way into the world, all 7 pounds 14 ounces of him.

He mastered the art of burping and bawling, went through a few diaper changes, then screwed up again. Whatever it takes to get rheumatic fever, he did it. Mom and Dad Wickman feared that was the last they'd hear of baby Floyd. But he fooled them. He recovered from the disease and went on to become a healthy kid.

That's the way it's always been with Floyd's life: First he screws up, then he tries again and succeeds. Write this down somewhere: Failure is the overture to success. If you don't fail, it means you aren't trying anything. If you aren't trying, you're not going to succeed. Floyd kept trying. Success didn't come to him. He had to go to it.

A HEAVENLY REJECT

You probably could look at that bout with rheumatic fever as a failure of sorts. I became a heavenly reject. You know how they always say at funerals, "God needed another flower for his heavenly bouquet, and so he picked a beautiful one from Earth." Only God left this flower on earth.

I was reminded of this brush with the Pearly Gates after one visit to the home of my sister. I found my little blonde niece, Jennifer, sitting on the porch steps, tears streaming from her precious blue eyes. In her lap was a shoe box.

I sat down beside her and put my arm around her.

"What's wrong, Honey," I asked.

"Fred died," she sobbed.

Fred was her pet turtle. I knew I had to say something to heal the hurt in her 6-year-old heart.

"Jennifer," I said, "You've been playing with Fred every day for six or eight months. Now God wants to play with him."

The look of sorrow in Jennifer's eyes turned to one of wonder.

"Uncle Floyd," she asked, "Why would God want to play with a dead turtle?"

Well, God didn't want to play with a dead Wickman. He pulled me through that bout with rheumatic fever and left me in the care and keeping of my mother and father.

When I got old enough to think about the matter, it occurred to me that my dad may not have looked upon me as a flower God left to grow and blossom. I thought it more likely that he saw me as a weed God didn't want messing up his bouquet. No matter how you add it up, you get a set of factors that contributed to a poor self-image. I wasn't geared toward thinking that maybe God said "I'm not ready for you yet; you've got good things to accomplish."

DON'T BLAME DAD

I don't go around knocking my dad. We're about as close now as a father and son can be. I've learned that if there's a problem standing between you and greatness, you can't overcome it by fixing the blame. You've got to fix the problem. If the problem is low self-esteem, you can't go running to your parents crying "You broke it, now put it back together." No matter who destroyed your self-esteem, only you can put it back together. It's useless blaming the past. Think of the past as a canceled check. It simply has no value.

Could my dad have helped with a little praise and support when I was growing up? Sure. But nobody's a perfect parent, and nobody gets a perfect childhood. Life deals each of us a hand and we have to play it. My dad played the hand he was dealt and I played the hand I was dealt. Parents can do all the right things to get their kids started in life and the kids can still screw up. It's all in how you play your hand.

My dad loved me when I was a kid; he just didn't always let on. He was like Freddie Hutchinson, the Detroit Tigers pitcher who went on to become a major-league manager. He was happy, but his face didn't know it. My dad seemed to find it hard to express love or appreciation. No matter what I would do, I would do it wrong, at least as he saw it. That was hard on the self-esteem. But it was not an excuse for giving up.

Do you feel as if nothing you do is good enough? Do you feel as though most others are better than you? If so, chances are you're living in the past. You should look to your past, learn from it, and let it go.

DAD THE PERFECTIONIST

For quite a few years, though, it did look as if Floyd had given up on himself. He never saw his father's perfectionist demands as challenges that would later sculpt his character. Instead, he saw them as impossible standards that he could never meet. He began to think of himself as a worthless weed as, time after time, he failed to measure up to his dad's expectations. In the elder Wickman's eyes, Floyd was born to screw up. You didn't get your "well done" from him until you did things perfectly. Floyd never did things perfectly.

Floyd and his dad didn't do father-and-son things together. The father never played catch with Floyd, or took him fishing, or out to see the Tigers or the Lions or the Red Wings. He didn't even go to high-school games when Floyd was struggling to stay on the team. So Floyd grew up with the feeling that his dad didn't care that much about him, and if his dad didn't care very much about him he must not be worth very much. By surrendering to that attitude, Floyd was setting himself up for failure.

STORMY HOME LIFE

Young Floyd's mom gave her children lots of love, but she and her husband had a stormy relationship. The elder Wickman had other loves in his life. Mostly they were aces, kings, and queens. And horses. His horses came around about as slowly as his aces, which meant that he was broke a lot. Mrs. Wickman was constantly threatening to kill herself or to leave him because he was running around or was gambling away his money. So the home often rang with the shouts of battling parents. The feeling of security and of belonging that is so vital to self-esteem in young children was lacking in Floyd's early surroundings.

LIFE IS NO MILK RUN

During Floyd's childhood, his closest relationship with his dad came about when Floyd would go with him on his Twin Pines Dairy milk route. Floyd was only about 7, but he was big enough to grab a carrier and run out to put the milk bottles by the doors.

You can imagine what a heady experience that was for a 7-year-old: helping to earn a living for the family.

But of course Floyd screwed up. At least he screwed up in his dad's eyes. He'd grab a carrier, scamper up to the door, and leave the specified number of milk bottles. He'd run back to the truck, hoping to hear his dad tell him what a good job he was doing.

"Jesus Christ," the father would say. "I told you to have the 'Twin Pines' facing the street. What kind of advertisement is it when people can't even tell what dairy it is that left the bottles? Now get the hell back up there and turn those bottles around."

Floyd's dad said "Jesus Christ" a lot—but rarely in prayer. It still offends Floyd when he hears those words. So from now on, we'll refer to the expression as "J---- C-----."

The elder Wickman was a real perfectionist on the milk route. A little lax when it came to cards and kids, but a perfectionist on the route.

Floyd didn't appreciate it at the time, but his dad was teaching him a valuable lesson: Do it right the first time. Yet it was also a negative kind of conditioning: The only way to be accepted was to do things perfectly. Nobody's perfect. Least of all little Floyd Wickman. So Floyd grew up thinking of himself as a mediocrity at best. He did not go into life with the image of Floyd Wickman, a man born for greatness.

When Floyd got a little older, he'd sometimes swing routes for other milkmen. Because his dad had conditioned him so well, he did a bang-up job for them. The milk got delivered and all the money was turned in. The other drivers were telling the old man what a great job his kid did. But never once did he come to Floyd and say, "Hey listen, Frank said you did a good job on his route." That would have done wonders for the boy's self-esteem, but it never happened.

DO THE THINGS YOU'RE GOOD AT DOING

If you want to build up your self-esteem, find something you're good at and get better at it—as good as you can get. If you want to keep your self-esteem down in the dumps, keep trying to be good at something you have no aptitude for.

If you stand six-feet-four and weigh 235 pounds, forget about riding a winner in the Kentucky Derby. If your self-esteem depends upon your success as a jockey, you won't even get out of the starting gate. If you're so awkward with your hands that you have trouble tying your shoes, do us all a favor and don't study to become a neurosurgeon. Your self-esteem will take a beating and your ineptitude may kill people.

If your voice sounds like two bricks rubbing together, don't try to boost your self-esteem through singing, no matter how much you admire Barbra Streisand or Luciano Pavoratti. If you're a girl with ordinary looks, don't go after the Miss Universe crown. Build your self-esteem in another area.

And if you're a kid with ordinary talents as an athlete, don't count on becoming a gridiron hero. Yes, you can try harder, and perhaps achieve a measure of success. But trying hard doesn't lead to greatness when you're trying hard at something you're not good at. Somebody who *is* good at it can try just as hard and leave you far behind. Your self-esteem will suffer and you will lose the zeal you need to go on to greatness.

FLOYD THE NON-ATHLETE

Floyd tried to become good at sports because he wanted to win his dad's approval. When the Wickman family would gather for Thanksgiving dinner at his grandmother's house, Floyd would envy his male cousins. They were athletic kids and Floyd wasn't. His dad would sit and talk to them about sports. Floyd was left out of those conversations.

It wasn't that the young Wickman didn't try. He would go out for every sport, trying to impress his dad. But it didn't work. He was still having to go out on the milk route, and that meant missing a lot of practices and a lot of school. Not that Floyd ever would have been a good football player. But he tried. Yet his dad never once came to a game. And Floyd never once saw himself as a successful athlete or a successful anything.

It showed when it came to other kinds of things. Floyd didn't try in school and later he didn't try in the Navy because he saw no point in it. He was a nobody, so why try to become somebody?

Floyd needed to recognize this fact: You don't have to be good at everything to be a "somebody." In later years, Floyd would discover talents in which he could take enormous pride.

How much better it would have been had he looked for, and found, those talents while he was growing up.

MAKE YOUR TALENT WORK FOR YOU

You have talent. Identify it and find a way to use it productively. Don't squander it on non-productive pursuits. If you have a good voice, don't waste it in the shower. By all means, develop it. Take voice lessons. Sing in public every time you get half an opportunity. Maybe you'll get that big break and become a star. Even if you don't get a recording contract, the applause of your friends will be a good morale booster.

If you're a carpenter and you have a talent for drawing, don't waste your talent on graffiti. Try your hand at designing things. Maybe you have the right stuff to become an architect or a furniture designer. But don't spend your life driving nails and wishing you were driving a Cadillac.

If you're a secretary to the marketing director and you have a flair for marketing promotions, develop that flair. If your job is washing windows and you yearn for a job that lets you dress in attractive fashions and that gives your nimble fingers a break from the cold water, learn to type and acquire the knowledge you need to become a secretary.

If you have a gift for gab, by all means use it to win friends and influence people. If it helps you get a date with the man or woman of your dreams, that's great. It can boost your self-esteem. But look for ways to put that gift to practical use as well.

GIRLS AND SELF-ESTEEM

Floyd wasn't good at athletics, and he wasn't good enough to please his dad on the milk route. So he concentrated his energies on the things he thought he was good at. Like finding girl friends.

Floyd's first marriage took place at the age of 7. Nancy Ellsmore and he got married in her garage. Floyd's older sister, Denise, came up with the idea. Nancy wore her communion dress and communion veil. Instead of walking down the aisle, she and Floyd walked together the two doors from the Wickman house to hers. In her garage was a big paper sign reading, "Just Married."

The kids weren't sure what married people did together, but they staged a big ceremony anyway. Needless to say, the marriage wasn't consummated. Some lessons come later in life. But from that time on, Floyd had a slew of girlfriends.

Going steady was the thing to do during the '40s and '50s. It meant committing yourself to one girl. Floyd went steady, but was never fanatical about his commitments. In fact, he often went steady with two or three girls at the same time. For him, girls were challenges. Having them wasn't important; what was important was getting them to the point that they liked him. Once he knew he could go steady with a girl, he really didn't have any interest in keeping the relationship going.

SELLING AND DATING

The dating game was probably his first opportunity to engage in a sales dialogue. He was selling himself.

"You wanna go steady?" he'd ask.

"Why do you wanna go steady? You've got a lot of girls."

"I don't want a lot of girls. I just want you."

Floyd was no Clark Gable, but it worked. The tools that would later carry him to greatness as a salesperson, a teacher and a motivator of people were there all along. But Floyd had not yet decided to use them productively, unless you consider a date with a cute girl to be a productive end use of your time and talents.

LOW SELF-ESTEEM WILL HOLD YOU BACK

Low self-esteem will keep you from putting your talents to their highest and best use. The goals you're capable of achieving seem out of reach. If you're a carpenter, you may have the inborn talent to achieve greatness as an architect. But your low self-esteem keeps telling you, "I'm not good enough to be an architect. That's an unrealistic dream." If you see yourself as a hired laborer instead of a talented professional, you will spend your life driving nails when you could be driving that Cadillac.

You may have the gift of persuasion that could enable you to charm a rhinoceros—the kind of gift that propels people to greatness in the sales arena. But if you see yourself as a paycheck slave, you'll never make the Million Dollar Club; never know the good things that your talents can bring you.

Low self-esteem severely restricts your comfort zone. It keeps you from going after goals that are well within your reach.

NOT IN BONNIE'S LEAGUE

Even when it came to the dating game, Floyd's low self-esteem held him back. Take the case of Bonnie. Bonnie was not the kind of girl Floyd Wickman normally took an interest in. She was smart, and athletic as well. She was also pretty, so Floyd tried his "sales" technique on her. It worked, for three dates. Then they broke up. The match wasn't meant to be. Bonnie seemed earmarked for success. Floyd was a cat. She was out of his comfort zone, and he didn't care to adjust to her values. Floyd didn't have the self-esteem necessary to play in her league.

DON'T LET IRRELEVANT FACTORS HOLD YOU BACK

Sometimes we let irrelevant things affect our self-esteem. Some people who come from poor or modest backgrounds are self-conscious about their origins. Even though they're loaded with talent, they feel that growing up in a walk-up apartment is a handicap that will keep them from competing with the country-club set. But some of the greatest success stories revolve around people who rose from humble beginnings. Abe Lincoln wasn't the only president who was born in a log cabin.

Any number of irrelevant factors may affect your self-esteem. Are you a man with low self-esteem because you stand only five-feet-seven? Napoleon was short too, but that didn't keep him from proclaiming himself emperor of France.

Did you grow up with a pronounced Brooklyn accent or a heavy Southern drawl? That's part of your past, and in most pursuits it's irrelevant. Lyndon Johnson rose to power in the Senate, then in the White House, while speaking in the heavy accents of a West Texan. Jimmy Carter's piping Georgia accent didn't keep him from the presidency. Tip O'Neill, the former speaker of the House, presided in the accents of a Boston Irishman. Many successful people are proud of their regional accents, but if you find yours a handicap, you can change it.

Before you let some supposed drawback murder your self-esteem, ask yourself: Does it matter? There have been many instances in my life that taught me the hard way that these drawbacks really don't matter.

AUTOMOBILES DON'T EQUAL SELF-ESTEEM

During Floyd Wickman's youth, cars were important to cats. This was Detroit, after all, and back then Detroit built automobiles. That was before the appearance of bumper stickers that read:

Hungry? Eat Your Toyota.

People were known by the cars they drove, and your self-esteem was closely tied in with the kind of wheels you were riding. If you were a kid, your self-esteem rose and fell with the status of the family car. Floyd's self-esteem therefore rode a roller-coaster.

One day his dad came home and said, "Come on, Floyd, let's go for a ride."

Floyd was game, as long as he didn't have to put milk bottles on doorsteps with the Twin Pines label facing the street.

They got into the family heap and drove to the Buick dealership in Centerline. There, sitting on the lot was the most beautiful automotive creation Floyd had ever seen. If Leonardo had designed it and Michelangelo had sculpted it, it couldn't have been more beautiful.

It was beige with light brown striping. It had that big, toothy grill that all Buicks had back then—that's probably where God got the inspiration for Jimmy Carter's mouth. The massive front bumpers had a couple of voluptuous bumper guards that would have made Blaze Starr envious. On the side of the front fenders were those chrome portholes that reminded you of a luxury yacht. They told you unmistakably: This is a Buick. Cadillacs had tail fins, Pontiacs had chrome streaks down the hood and deck lid, and Buicks had portholes. Everybody knew that.

In the '50s, when only the textile industry was afraid of Japan and when foreign cars were called "bugs" and could barely climb American-class hills, Buick was **The** *American car. Cadillac was the ultimate, of course. A Buick was to a Cadillac what a Bentley was to a Rolls. It was the car for the person who had arrived but didn't want to announce it with blaring trumpets. Though it dripped with chrome and bulged with opulence, compared to the Cadillac it was an understatement.*

But this Buick had a crowning touch that made it special. Bringing up the rear was a continental spare—a dressy but sporty add-on guaranteed to catch the eye of every girl at Jefferson Beach.

All Floyd could do was gape, while his dad stood there grinning broadly, as if he'd just topped somebody's straight with a flush.

"Man, check that continental spare!" Floyd gasped.

"And she's got Dynaflow and power steering," said the salesman, grinning like a man who had just earned a commission. "And a four-barrel carb, with twin exhausts. They're putting V-8s in 'em now."

The elder Wickman didn't know a four-barrel carb from four aces, and he probably thought Dynaflow was a new soft drink. But Floyd knew what it meant, and every cat in his neighborhood knew.

"Put a set of glasspacks on her, and I'll bet she'd stay even with an Eighty-Eight," Floyd said. The Olds 88 was the family hot-rod of its era—the standard by which every other car's performance was measured.

"Get in and let's drive her home," said his dad.

Floyd couldn't believe his ears. This fantastic blend of luxury, performance and utter cool was going to be parked in the Wickman driveway. Maybe when he got his driver's license he could borrow it to take Nancy to the drive-in.

That Buick was a part of their lives for two weeks. One day Floyd came home from school and found in its place a run-of-the-mill old Ford. He knew what had happened. His dad's horse had arrived late again, and the Buick payments had flown out the betting window. It wouldn't be the last sharp car that would be parked in their driveway for a few weeks, then disappear in a stack of lost chips. It wouldn't be the last time Floyd's self-esteem would take a beating because it depended more on the car he was in than it did on what was in Floyd. But Floyd eventually realized that all this was irrelevant. So what if his dad had to give up his Buick and go back to a Ford? Today, Floyd has a fleet of Cadillac limousines at his disposal. They're one of his business sidelines. They make money for him, and they add to his self-esteem.

SHED NO TEARS

All this talk about problems of growing up is not intended to win your sympathy. You don't need to pat me on the head and say, "Poor Floyd; no wonder it took you so long to find your bearings." Others have had a lot tougher childhoods than I had, and they found themselves a lot quicker.

As Nido Qubein, a colleague of mine in High Point, North Carolina, expressed it in his book, *Get the Best from Yourself:*

> What matters is not so much how you got to be the way you are now, but what you do with the person you

> have become. There is nothing helpful in blaming your parents, the way society has treated you, your physical or mental limitations, or anything else, for things you don't like about yourself. The real issues are: Who are you. What are you going to do with yourself.[1]

I was 26 years old before I decided what I was going to do with myself. The reason it took so long is that I made what seemed to be a trivial decision when I was in my early teens. I decided to become a cat, and that decision fixed my self-image. I did not see myself as a person capable of making a solid contribution to society. That was just the opposite of what a cat was supposed to do. I did not see myself as a person entitled to the good things in life. At least in my mind, those things were like my smart and athletic girlfriend, Bonnie: out of my league and out of my reach. I was like the vagabond standing on a street corner watching a large stretch limousine pass by. In the back seat was a well-groomed, successful-looking gentleman. Out loud, for the world to hear, the vagabond announced, "But for me, there go I."

THE SELF-IMAGE WAS DECEPTIVE

Such was my self-image at one time. Never mind that this self-image was deceptive. I believe I have made a solid contribution to society, sharing both my wealth and my expertise with others. I have enjoyed the good things in life, including a beautiful and intelligent wife, three fine sons and whatever I desire in material possessions.

I did not become, at the age of 26, a different individual. I

---

[1]Nido R. Qubein, *Get the Best from Yourself,* (Englewood Cliffs, New Jersey: Prentice-Hall, Inc, 1983) pp. 42–43.

simply realized that I could put aside the old self-image and replace it with a new one. The lessons in life became clear, and I started the **Seven-Step** process.

A bad self-image can be a screen that shuts out the view of an entire world of opportunity. Maybe you screened yourself off from success through a similar decision taken during your formative years. If you did, get it out of the way fast. I took my time about it. Read on to see what happened.

RUNNING WITH THE GANG

It was about 1954, when he turned 13, that Floyd graduated from screwing up milk deliveries to screwing up royally. He reached adolescence with that poor self-image that told him that he wasn't smart enough or rich enough to excel as a square. Nor did he come from the right kind of family. He was not the pampered child of rich parents. His self-esteem had never been fed on stories of family successes, of illustrious ancestors, of prestigious relatives. His family folklore consisted of Mom's tirades against Dad for gambling away a good salary. His model of success was a milk bottle on the doorstep with the Twin Pines label facing the street.

He did not draw self-esteem from his family, because success was not a family tradition, although there were some relatives who seemed to do quite well for themselves. He didn't draw it from within himself, because he was always fouling things up, which meant he was imperfect. Imperfection, as his dad constantly taught him on the milk route, was unacceptable.

As we have seen, all these family factors were, in reality, irrelevant. But Floyd had not yet learned that. He had within him and around him other sources of self-esteem, if only he had realized it. But to a young cat on the streets of Detroit's

East Side in 1954, only one seemed relevant. Floyd started running with gangs.

By today's standards, Floyd's gang was pretty innocent. El Duches didn't mug and rape. They didn't hold satanic rites. You weren't required to kill somebody to become a member of the gang. Mostly, they broke windows, got into fist fights with other gangs, committed petty larceny, and often went joy riding in stolen cars.

THE IMAGE OF A LOSER

If you're still taking notes, write this down: If you think like a loser, you'll be a loser. You tend to live up to—or down to—your image of yourself. My dad's steadfast refusal to acknowledge any of my positive achievements had left me with a loser's self-image. When you think so little of yourself, even stealing is not a big come-down. If you were a cat and a member of the gang, stealing stuff, breaking windows, getting into gang fights was a natural part of living, just as getting up and going to work on the assembly line was a natural thing for the auto workers around Detroit.

THE PITFALLS OF CAR THEFT

Floyd was 14 when he took part in his first car theft. He was with Tom, Scotty and Bill. They had hitchhiked to Jefferson Beach on Lake St. Clair, northeast of Detroit. It was too far to walk and too expensive to take the bus. It got too late for hitchhiking back, so they swiped a car, drove it around for several hours, then left it in the middle of a Detroit street.

After that, it got easier. Floyd had the thief's self-image and stealing cars was no longer a big deal. But the easier an unhealthy practice becomes, the deeper your involvement in it. Sooner or later, you're going to be in over your head. Floyd helped steal about a dozen cars before he got caught.

It happened the night Floyd's steady girlfriend, Judy, threw a party. Jack and Floyd were going to the party together. Detroit was in a deep chill. Judy lived six blocks off the main thoroughfare and it would be a cold walk. So the boys decided to "borrow" a car for the evening.

They parked it a block or two from Judy's house. After the party, they walked back to the car. As Jack was hot-wiring the ignition, a police car pulled up.

"Let's go, Jack," Floyd hissed, as he broke and ran down the street.

The voice from the squad car crackled like gunfire.

"Stop!"

Floyd kept running, but he turned to look over his shoulder.

The cop was standing with feet apart, his gun extended toward the boy.

"If you don't stop, I'll shoot."

"Don't shoot! Don't shoot!" Floyd shouted, and he ran to the cop as if the policeman were his long-lost friend.

Down at Conners Precinct, the cops called Floyd's dad and told him to come and get his son.

Floyd expected fire and brimstone, but what he got was rather mild.

"J---- C-----," his dad said, using his all-purpose expression. It was almost as if the father wasn't interested in what the son had done. He didn't take Floyd to the woodshed and he didn't take away his allowance. What's an allowance? What's a woodshed?

The cops must have figured the boys were just up to some harmless joy-riding. They let them go without punishment. But Floyd's name went into the book.

The upshot was that he went to live with his sister Jackie and her husband George, who was a cop. Ironically, they lived in St. Clair Shores, the site of Floyd's first auto theft.

"You've got to get away from that gang," Floyd's mother told him.

Poor Mom. How could she know that a little thing like having a cop for a brother-in-law could not separate a cat from his gang? And a trip to the precinct was not going to shame Floyd into mending his ways. He had the self-image of a gang member. He was what he was, and he wasn't going to change.

NINTH-GRADE FAILURE

By the time he reached the ninth grade, Floyd had already flunked two grades. No big deal. A cat isn't supposed to be a scholar. School is a place a cat goes to until he's old enough to quit. Floyd was 15 ½ years old and on his way to becoming the only ninth grader at Denby High School who had to shave every day.

He was going with Audrey that year, and the school was operating on a staggered schedule. That meant that Audrey was in school while Floyd was out, and he was in school while she was out.

Floyd soon caught on to another convenient detail: Audrey's parents were not home during the hours when he was in school and Audrey was out.

It didn't take him long to figure out that Audrey's living room was a lot more fun to be in than any classroom at Denby.

One day Floyd showed up at school, just to make sure the place was still there.

The home-room teacher seemed surprised to see him.

"Welcome back," she said. "I think the principal would like to see you."

Floyd was every inch the cat as he walked into the principal's office.

"Where've you been?" the principal asked. From his look and his tone, Floyd knew it wasn't a friendly inquiry.

"Oh, round and about."

"Well, our records show that you haven't been around and about the school. You've been absent for 40 straight days. What have you been doing?"

"I dunno. Just goofing off, I guess."

"Do your parents know you've been goofing off?"

"I don't think so."

"Well, they're about to find out," he said. "They send you here to get an education. We can't educate you if you don't show up for class. I don't know what you've been doing all the time you were supposed to be in school, but I can tell you one thing: There's a school-attendance law in this state, and you're going to go to school one way or another. It's up to you to decide: You can go to this one, where the doors are open and you can walk in and walk out. Or you can go to another one, where they put locks on the doors and you won't have a key."

Floyd didn't really believe him. But he figured his dad and mom would take some sort of action.

"J---- C-----," said the elder Wickman when he heard the news.

For some reason Floyd thought he was going to say that.

NO CHEERS FOR NOTRE DAME

"Do you think they can do anything for him at Notre Dame High School?" asked Mrs. Wickman.

"All they can do is try," said her husband.

Golda Meir used to say that Moses wasn't such a smart guy. He led the Israelites around in the wilderness for 40 years before taking them to the only spot in the Middle East that didn't have oil.

Well, Floyd's 40 days in the wilderness of Detroit was about as fruitful. He ended up at another place where he wouldn't get an education.

Notre Dame was a great school, dedicated to all the enlightened principles of Torquemada. Floyd would later reflect that, in all his years of attending parochial schools, he never had a teacher to take a personal interest in him. They seated the pupils alphabetically, and since Wickman came under the "W's," Floyd was always in the back of the room—out of sight, out of mind.

But one teacher did pay attention to him. His name was Mr. Cyr and he taught science. While he was explaining how the ice sheets came and went during the Pleistocene era, Pete and Floyd were discussing the relative merits of the Chevrolet Bel Aire and the Ford Fairlane 500.

Mr. Cyr turned from the blackboard.

"Perhaps Floyd would like to come forward and tell us how the Great Lakes were formed," he said.

Floyd hadn't the foggiest notion of how the Great Lakes were formed. He hesitated while he tried to collect his thoughts.

"I said come up to the front of the classroom!" There was a trace of rage in Mr. Cyr's voice.

Floyd had worn motorcycle boots to class, which was what you'd expect a cat to wear. He had taken them off to get comfortable, and as he walked toward the front of the room, he was pulling them on.

He was looking down at his boot when he felt the crack of Mr. Cyr's knuckles against his head. Floyd went to the floor. The teacher kept beating him. Floyd knew he wasn't long for that school.

CAUGHT AGAIN

Not long after that, Floyd got caught again for taking part in a car theft. Actually, he had nothing to do with stealing the car. He happened to accept a ride home from the guys who did steal it.

Floyd had gone to a Harper Woods High School basketball game. After the game, Scotty drove up in a beautiful white '56 Chevrolet convertible, and there was Jack in the front seat beside him. It might as well have had "stolen car" written all over it.

"C'mon Floyd, let's take her for a spin."

"Not tonight, Scotty. I ain't looking for no trouble."

"Get with it, pal. This baby is loaded for bear. She's got twin carbs and dual exhausts. Open 'er up and you're flying low."

"I can't do it, man. It'll just get me in trouble."

"C'mon, Floyd. Just a short ride."

Floyd hesitated a second. Then: "Well, okay, if you'll just drop me off at Jackie's house."

So they dropped him off at his sister's and he watched them drive away.

Next day at school, somebody came to the classroom where Floyd was sitting.

"Floyd Wickman's wanted in the office."

When he got there, he saw two big cops.

"You're wanted for auto larceny," they said.

At the police station, Floyd learned what had happened.

"Understand you were seen in a sharp white Chevy convertible the other night," said the cop.

"I went for a ride with a friend. I figured it was his car."

"Who was your friend."

"I don't know his name. He just picked me up at the basketball game and took me home."

"Nice friend you've got. You don't know his name, huh?"

"No sir."

"Well, he knows yours."

"Then he knows me better than I know him."

"His name is Scotty, and he has a friend named Jack. In

fact, Jack's a friend of both of you. He says you and him and Scotty all went riding in that stolen convertible.''

''I didn't know it was stolen.''

''Yeah, yeah, and Santa Claus doesn't know when it's Christmas.''

''Look kid, this isn't the first time for you. You've been caught before with a stolen car. And I'll bet there have been a lot of times when you weren't caught. This time, you're going before the judge. Merry Christmas.''

CHRISTMAS IN DETENTION

Floyd landed in detention home down on Forest Avenue and he had to stay for the duration of the Christmas season.

Jackie and Mom came to visit on Christmas Eve. Floyd remembered past Christmases when the family was all together. There was something about the holiday season that brought extra warmth into the home, and Floyd missed it something terrible.

He thought about the tree and the presents and the family camaraderie. Then he thought about the evening before him, in a room alone with 50 other troublemakers, any of whom could steal him blind or beat him to a pulp without remorse.

Floyd hugged his mother and sister. Then he saw the door close behind them. From a window he watched them walk back to their car. God, how he wanted to go with them. There they were, free to go home, to enjoy the eggnog and the carols and the presents in the festive glow of Christmas lights. Here he was, locked away from all of that, confined to a cheerless room full of cheerless punks. That was the day Floyd quit being a thief.

"YOUR SON IS A LOSER"

After the holidays, they let him go home. He didn't go back to Notre Dame High School. Instead, he enrolled in Osborne High—his third school that year.

Detention didn't make a scholar out of him, but the principal, Mr. Holt, did him a big favor. He told Floyd's mother, "Your son is a loser."

Those words stuck with Floyd and provided a great deal of the motivation that drove him to success.

What Mr. Holt said was certainly true at the time. Although detention home had scared the car thievery out of him, it had done nothing to raise his self-esteem. His world was still the streets of Detroit, and he could not see himself breaking out of this environment and rubbing elbows with top executives in the business world, much less teaching other people how to be successful.

CODEINE, VALO AND BOOZE

Floyd quit school the day he turned 16. He had already been helping his dad on the milk route a lot. He had also worked at a super market. He was a good worker. He was getting nowhere fast in school, so he just quit.

That was when he really started to screw up. It's a wonder the next year didn't screw him up for life. He started getting into alcohol and dope.

Floyd wasn't into the kind of drugs kids do today. He never got into heroin or cocaine or LSD, and of course nobody had heard about crack. His "drugs" consisted of Valo nose inhaler and Cosinel cough medicine.

The Cosinel contained codeine. He'd guzzle it until he got a euphoric high.

The Valo packed a different kind of wallop. Floyd would break open the container, and inside would be a piece of cotton about the size of a cigarette. It was soaked with a liquid that was supposed to clear the sinuses. He'd chop the cotton into seven parts and swallow it with a bottle of wine. Between the wine and the inhaler, he'd be as high as a kite for 48 hours. There was nothing pleasing about this, except that it made Floyd feel like he could take on anybody and anything.

Floyd was not a happy kid in those days. He thought nobody liked him. That's what a negative self-image can do for you. You don't like yourself, so you figure nobody likes you. It was a feeling bred into him during those milk-route days when nothing he did seemed to please his dad. Floyd couldn't feel his father's love, so he figured he wasn't loved. He had to earn love by doing things perfectly, and he could never do things perfectly. So why try?

BUILDING YOUR SELF-ESTEEM

If your self-esteem suffers from that kind of early experience, it can be built up. When you're feeling down on yourself, what makes you feel better?

A little praise and encouragement can do wonders. So to build up your self-esteem, you need to cultivate a circle of friends who will give you that praise and encouragement.

You don't find these friends by going from bar to bar and saying, "Won't somebody please say something nice about me?" To find those friends who will praise you, you first want to find out what you can do that is worthy of praise.

Look for the things that you're truly gifted in. You're good at something. Find out what it is. Then make up your mind to be as good at it as you possibly can. As you begin to improve your skills, you will come into contact with people who share your interest. They will praise your progress and pretty soon you'll find your self-esteem rising.

Maybe your strength is in athletics. There are amateur leagues in which you can play or coach. Maybe it's music. The person who can play a decent guitar or piano is always in demand on social occasions. Maybe it's designing clothes or repairing cars or building things or helping out at the volunteer rescue squad.

You may excel at a hobby or at a vocation. But find what it is that you're good at and determine to get better at it. You'll find yourself drawing an admiring circle of friends around you, and their compliments will boost your self-esteem.

BREAK OUT OF THE LOSER'S CIRCLE

I chose a circle of friends who would encourage me to goof off. I ran with a street gang, and so I acquired the self-image of a gang member. So as a teen-ager, I had no goals, no ambitions, no plans for the future. I had a history of failure. I was facing some bad odds.

If you're aimless and unsuccessful—no matter what your age—take a look at your circle of friends. Are they the people who will encourage you to succeed? Or will they reinforce your poor self-image?

If all your friends are failures, you're going to be a failure too. Otherwise you won't belong to the group.

Suppose you find yourself in the middle of a wilderness among friends who are as lost as you are. You know there's a road out there somewhere, and you know you've got to find it if you expect to reach shelter by nightfall. But your friends are dawdling, playing hide and seek with each other, meandering up side trails, chasing chipmunks through the underbrush.

You spot a group of hikers who are walking briskly and confidently in a steady direction. You're hungry and you know that soon it's going to be dark and cold.

Do you stick with your dawdling friends, or do you fall into step with the hikers?

This doesn't mean you have to turn your back on your friends to succeed.

It means that you have to widen your circle of friendships. You have to look for people who know where they're going, and get into step with them.

If your old friends choose to string along with you, fine. You've helped them find their direction.

If they choose to part company, count it their loss. You want to move on—away from the old, aimless environment and toward the greatness that is rightfully yours.

You can do that only if you have a high opinion of yourself. You can't become a winner so long as you go around with a loser's attitude. You can't start taking those **Seven Steps** to Greatness until you are convinced that you have within you the stuff of greatness.

Floyd Wickman is here to tell you that you have the stuff of greatness. This is not blind faith on my part. I know it. The moment when you know it too is the moment you will start taking the steps to live up to your new self-image. The moment you start **thinking** like a winner is the moment you will start **acting** like a winner.

So as you start on the road to greatness, remember what I learned the slow, hard way: If you're going to succeed, you've got to believe in yourself. Nobody ever arrived at the top with a bad self-image.

List the most important points you have gained from the preceding Lesson:

Lesson Three

If You Don't Know What You Want, Mediocrity Is What You'll Get

If you want to achieve greatness, you have to know what you're looking for. You won't find it by wandering aimlessly through life waiting to stub your toe on success. You're more likely to stumble into the quicksand of mediocrity.

Most people who end up as mediocrities do so because they drift through life without planning. They have no purpose other than to live from paycheck to paycheck, buying the groceries, paying the rent and holding off the bill collectors.

It isn't that they're not smart or that they lack energy. You can work like a slave day in and day out and never pull yourself out of the rut you're in. Why? Because your energy is being wasted. You're not directing it toward a purpose.

When you have a purpose in life, then you tend to focus your energy on the things that move you toward that purpose.

When you have no purpose, all your energy is like water going over a dam. It falls onto the rocks below, and it rushes on downstream, but it doesn't accomplish a thing. There is no purpose behind it.

But when you take the same amount of water and run it through a turbine, it produces the electricity that lights cities and runs factories. It has acquired a purpose.

So ask yourself now: "What do I want to do with my life?" Look within yourself. What kind of activity gives you the greatest satisfaction? What kind of activity do you have a special talent for? What good can you accomplish for yourself and humanity by pursuing this activity?

The highest purpose, and the one most likely to lead you to greatness, is one that enables you to benefit others. This doesn't mean that you have to deprive yourself and your family to achieve greatness. It means simply that when you put yourself at the service of mankind, mankind tends to pay you for services rendered. Look at the great success stories of our era. Thomas Edison electrified the country and made a fortune in the bargain. Henry Ford put America on wheels and made millions. George Eastman made it possible for every family to have its own album of memories, and he became rich. Tom Monaghan made it possible for people to enjoy good pizza without leaving their homes, and he's rolling in the dough. Humanity would be the poorer without the advances these men brought. And neither of them went to the poorhouse because of the services they rendered.

Find a purpose that will benefit your fellow man. Aim high, then put your energy to work toward that purpose.

DRIFTING INTO THE NAVY

Floyd Wickman entered the Navy with no higher purpose than to get away from Detroit and put some excitement in his life. He still didn't know what he wanted, and so he remained mired in mediocrity.

Floyd had wasted his teen years in meaningless activity designed to secure his status as a cat. He had avoided anything that looked like academic achievement. On his 16th birthday, he had dropped out of school.

After that, Floyd headed downhill fast. He did a lot of drinking and "hanging out" with the gang. In fact, he was drunk a great deal of the time during that first year out of school. On his 17th birthday, Floyd, Dale, and Buster were hanging out trying to get a handle on who they were and where they were going.

"I'm sick of this town," said Floyd. "I hate being at home. I hate hanging out at the hamburger joint. I hate being high; I hate being sober. I hate it when I screw up everything I do. Hell, I can't even shoot a decent game of pinball."

"So whatta you gonna do?"

"I dunno. **Go** *somewhere, I guess.*

"And where you gonna go? Roseville? Grosse Pointe? Ferndale?

"Nah. I mean **GO** *somewhere."*

"Like Toledo?"

"Like England or Africa or China."

That broke the other two up.

"Yeah, yeah," said Buster. "So let's go down to Roy O'Brien's used-car lot and swipe a car. We can take turns driving it to Africa."

"I was thinking about joining the Navy," Floyd said. "Friend of mine said it's a ball. You get to go to all these ports where there's beaches and bars and babes all over the place. He says

they really go for guys in Navy uniforms. And in some of those places you can buy rum cheaper than you can buy Pepsi."

"You serious?" asked Dale.

"Why not? It beats the hell out of sitting around this place and watching the pavement crack."

So they all went down to the Navy recruiting office, and there was this guy in a petty officer's uniform—though Floyd didn't know what a petty officer was at the time.

"How old are you?" he asked.

"Seventeen."

"What grade are you in?"

"I've been out of school for a year."

"Okay. The Navy can use you, but you're going to have to get your parents to sign for you."

Floyd's dad signed in a heartbeat. His mom tried to talk him out of it.

"You've never been away from home, Floyd."

"I know, Mom. That's why I'm joining the Navy. I want to see what the rest of the world looks like."

"But what if we go to war? Haven't you seen those movies where the ships get bombed or those suicide bombers dive into the decks."

"It's 1958, Mom. Japan's not going to fight us any more. It's been five years since the Korean War. And if the Russians decide to fight us, they're not going to waste their atomic bombs on a ship. They're going to drop them on Detroit and New York."

Mrs. Wickman finally gave in. Perhaps she figured that the Navy might be able to do for Floyd what Notre Dame High School had failed to do.

Floyd showed up for induction alone. Dale and Buster decided they could do without the beaches, bars and babes. They'd settle for Detroit.

THE SERVICES CAN'T TELL YOU WHAT YOU WANT

The armed forces can be the salvation of young people who want to take advantage of what they can offer—and who are willing to take the risk of being involved in a shooting war.

The services offer structure, discipline and training that can be valuable preparation for civilian life. They also offer good career opportunities and chances for greatness.

But greatness comes only to those who know what they want. If you want to make the military your career, you focus your energy and efforts on acquiring the knowledge and skills necessary to advance. If you acquire that purpose while still in high school, you can try to make it into one of the military academies. Or you may join the ROTC in college. Or you may enlist and aim for Officer Candidate School.

Kids who walk aimlessly into recruiting offices and drift aimlessly into the enlisted ranks will sink aimlessly into mediocrity—until they decide what they want from life.

AN AIMLESS DECADE

The Navy was Floyd Wickman's life for most of the next decade. He didn't exactly become another Bull Halsey. Instead, he became a storekeeper aboard a cruiser. There isn't a lot of glory in being a storekeeper aboard a small ship. But at least it took him away from the Cosinel, the Valo and the booze. The Navy was a place to drift until he could get his bearings.

Irving Berlin wrote a light-hearted lyric about the Navy:

We joined the Navy
to see the world;

And what did we see?
We saw the sea.

But first Floyd saw boot camp at Great Lakes, Illinois. That's where he landed on October 20, 1958. Winter was already in the air, but he didn't care. He was on his way to adventure, far from the streets of Detroit. He was also on his way to failure—the first time around. He didn't know you could flunk boot camp, but he flunked it.

IT TAKES EDUCATION

Even in boot camp, you experience the drawbacks of an aimless life. To get ahead in the modern Navy, you have to be able to do other things besides swab decks. Most of these other things require education.

You don't get that education by just showing up at school and acting cool. You get it by purposefully studying, acquiring the knowledge that will help you do what you want to do with your life. That's what squares did back in the '50s. Cats wouldn't dream of studying for a career. Cats couldn't think beyond those teen years. To them, life was just one long period of adolescence. If you asked them what they wanted to be when they grew up, they couldn't tell you. Not knowing what they wanted, they became mediocrities.

Knowing how to walk and talk and stare like a cat didn't help at all when it came to breaking into the Navy. Nor did knowing how to hot-wire a car in the dark for the purpose of joy riding.

What did count was knowledge—the kind you picked up in the classroom. The Navy, of all things, expected its recruits to be reasonably literate and to know their math.

FLUNKING BOOT CAMP

Floyd did not have the knowledge the Navy was looking for. He hadn't learned to read well and he hadn't learned to study. So instead of making it through boot camp in eight weeks, he had to stay for 12 just to get past the scholastic requirements.

Even so, he enjoyed it, which is odd. You're not supposed to like boot camp.

FACING A DULL ROUTINE

When you know what you want to do, and you make up your mind to do it, it's amazing what you can do. But first you have to know what you want to do.

Let's say you're a salesperson. You get up in the morning feeling bright and energetic. You have your breakfast, watch a little morning television, and breeze to work. You haven't given the first thought to what you want to accomplish that day.

You know you have a major presentation to make that afternoon. You know there are a dozen or so referrals you need to follow up on. You know of one prospect who appears to be one or two calls away from closing. You know you ought to be using your telephone book and city directory to scout for prospects. You know you have a stack of order forms to fill out. And you know you have to get to work on your monthly sales report.

Will you spend your morning preparing for the presentation, or will you try to wing it? Will you spend the morning trying to set up appointments with some of the referrals? Will you try to nail down that prospect who's close to closing? Will you spend your day trying to develop leads through the phone book and city directory? Or will you get to work on those orders and that sales report?

If you don't know what you want to do, you'll end up doing nothing very well. You'll come to the end of the day feeling tired and frustrated. You will have expended energy, but the energy will not have been focused.

The salesperson with a purpose would not have waited until arrival at the office to decide what to do. That afternoon's presentation would have long ago been prepared and rehearsed. There would be time slots set aside for each of the other things needed to keep business coming in.

And each of those things would have been accomplished in its own due time.

Maybe preparing presentations, setting up appointments or dialing cold prospects isn't the most exciting activity you can pursue. But when you have a purpose in mind, you find ways of livening up the dull routine. It was one of the lessons I learned in boot camp, though I didn't really put it to use until years later, after I had acquired a larger purpose.

In boot camp, you didn't have to fill out orders or compile sales reports. But you had to wash GI cans. I knew what I had to do, and I found a way to take the drudgery out of doing it.

THE CAN-WASHING GAME

During boot camp, Floyd and another recruit drew the assignment to clean out all the GI cans in their unit. It was raw cold outside, and both of them had enlisted with the idea of sailing into tropical ports that were teeming with beautiful babes waiting to welcome them ashore. They hadn't bargained for hosing out dirty cans in the frosty air of an Illinois winter.

The sailor's vocabulary of profanity is legendary, and Floyd's companion was halfway through the dictionary when Floyd stopped him.

''Hey, don't get so bent out of shape,'' said the kid from Detroit. ''Where you from?''

''Columbus, Ohio,'' replied the other recruit.

''Columbus, huh? Don't they have a school there called Ohio State or something? Can guys from Ohio clean cans any better than they can play football?''

''Whatta you talking about?''

''I'm from Michigan, and we don't take second place to Buckeyes in nothing. I'll bet I can clean more of these than you can.''

''Oh yeah? Who won the last Rose Bowl?'' asked the Buckeye.

''Against Oregon State, who could lose? But this ain't the Rose Bowl and I ain't Oregon State. When it comes to cleaning cans, a Michigander can beat a Buckeye any day.''

''Like hell you can.''

It didn't matter who won the contest. Floyd had turned it into a game. In the process of having fun, the two recruits got the dirty job done.

Little incidents like that demonstrate that Floyd had some positive things going for him if he cared to exploit them. It's not every guy who will take the trouble to make a game out of cleaning GI cans in subfreezing weather.

SURVIVING THE SETBACKS

Knowing what you want enables you to put your disappointments in perspective. If you have a long-range purpose, you can view day-to-day setbacks as minor bumps on the way to your destination. You can make the best of them, then move on toward your goal. This is true even when it comes to courtship, as I learned in another boot-camp experience.

DEAR JOHN, DEAR JANE

Floyd hadn't been in boot camp long before he experienced a test of his capacity to rise above disappointments. It wasn't an earth-shattering event, though Floyd thought it was at the time. Lynn wrote him a Dear John letter.

Floyd had been going with Lynn for a while, and sailors always like to know there's a girl back home, even when they're whooping it up with a different girl in every port.

But maybe it's too much to expect a teen-aged sweetheart to stay faithful to a cat who has left her in favor of the Seven Seas.

When Floyd got the letter, he thought of calling Lynn and using all his cool charm to win her back. But it wasn't in his nature to go crawling. He decided that she wasn't going to get the better of him. So that very same day, he wrote ***her*** *a Dear Jane letter. He wrote it as if he had never received her letter; as if the two had crossed in the mail. He never knew whether she bought the deception or not. But it made him feel good.*

NO PRIORITIES

The episode with Lynn would have hurt less had I had a clear picture of where I was going with my life. Seventeen is a bit young to center your life on one person of the opposite sex. The kid with his life under control would have reasoned that these were the years when you played the field, enjoying the company of a variety of people until finally you had settled on the qualities you wanted in a spouse. Then, once you knew what you wanted, you set out to find that one ideal partner for life. Viewed in this perspective, Lynn was a girl with whom I'd had some good times. Her letter closed the door on that relationship, but opened the door to many others that I could enjoy until the right woman came along. In time, the right woman came along. She wasn't Lynn.

Why didn't the Navy recognize all these positive traits in me? It would have had I made the Navy my first priority in life. But how could I make it my first priority when I didn't even have any priorities? How could I have priorities when I didn't know what I wanted?

The aimless ways of the cat on the streets of Detroit continued during the Navy years.

BACK TO THE GANGS

From Great Lakes, the Navy shipped Floyd to Maryland, where he was assigned to an air squadron for a while. Then he was assigned to the cruiser Galveston *for a couple of years.*

When he came aboard, the Galveston *was at the Philadelphia Naval Shipyard for an overhaul. She stayed there for 10 months before putting out to sea.*

In all the old movies, the Navy is full of clean-cut but lusty young lads who do a lot of hell-raising on shore but are true to the core when they're among their shipmates.

Seaman Floyd Wickman didn't follow that script. The fact is, he didn't hang around with any of the sailors. He took the subway into town and hung out with a gang over on Spring Garden Street. It was worse than the gang in Detroit. They would sleep in roach-infested apartments, a far cry from Jackie and George's digs in St. Clair Shores. Floyd was involved in two gang fights while he was in Philly. Needless to say, advancement came slowly.

KNOWING WHAT TO DO WITH SUCCESS

When you know what you want, you are prepared to deal with the successes that come your way. When you're blundering aimlessly, even your successes can crumble in your hands.

When many people think of success, they think in terms of winning a multimillion-dollar lottery, or striking it rich in some other painless fashion. But they don't think beyond the winning. They think they want wealth, but they soon discover that wealth means nothing unless you have a purpose in life. We've all read about athletes or entertainers who struck it rich without any concept of what they wanted to do with their riches. Because they didn't know what they wanted to do, they didn't plan. And because they didn't plan, their money was soon gone and the IRS was knocking on their door.

Joe Louis, the great heavyweight fighter, had to go into the ring long after his prime in order to earn the money to pay the taxes on income he had already spent or lost.

We have also heard of lottery winners who ended up sadly broke after aimlessly running through their fortunes. Because they didn't know what they wanted, they were unable to achieve greatness, even with the head start a few million dollars can give you.

I discovered, on a much smaller scale, that receiving something for nothing is a blessing only if you know what you're getting and know what you want to do with it. The lesson was conveyed through a 50-cent automobile.

THE FOUR-BIT CHEVROLET

It happened while Floyd was in the Navy. While he was home on leave, he got his driver's license. All those times he had been joy-riding in "borrowed" cars, he had been driving without a license. Now that he could drive a car lawfully, he needed a lawful car to drive. He picked one up for 50 cents. A steal? Not quite.

Tyrone Johnson, a strapping seaman on the Galveston, *had a '49 Chevrolet he wanted to get rid of. It was a clunker, and if the gang back in Detroit had been out to swipe a car for a bit of joy riding they wouldn't have given this one a second glance. On a used-car lot it would have brought $200 tops.*

Well, Tyrone needed more than $200, so he hit upon an idea. He raffled the old Chevy off for 50 cents a ticket. He must have made $1,000 off that worn-out car. Floyd won the raffle.

When he took possession of the car, Floyd gave no thought to the kind of shape it was in or what it would require to operate it legally. To think about that would be to put some direction into his life. Floyd's life had no direction. He still didn't know where he was going or where he wanted to go.

Floyd immediately took the car for a drive across Philadelphia. The old heap was chugging along real good when he glanced into his rearview mirror and saw a flashing light. He wasn't speeding and the car wasn't stolen, so he didn't know what was up.

"Where's your inspection sticker?" asked the cop.

"I didn't know you had to have one."

"Every car in the state of Pennsylvania has to have a safety inspection," he growled. "I'm writing you out a ticket for not having an inspection sticker. You'd better go get this crate inspected before you get another ticket. This can get expensive, you know."

Floyd accepted the ticket and continued on his aimless way. He was almost across Philly, still cursing his luck, when he saw another red light blinking in his rear-view. This time he was ready.

"I realize I don't have an inspection sticker, officer," he

said. "But one of your buddies across town has already stopped me and given me this ticket. So if you don't mind, I'd like to get back to my ship."

The cop slowly gave the decrepit old Chevy the once-over.

"This car must have been through hell since my buddy across town gave you this ticket," he said sarcastically. "Your muffler's so loud they can hear you in Jersey. And who put that crack in your windshield? I'm going to give you a ticket for a faulty muffler and obstructed vision. You get smart with me and I can come up with so many violations you'll have to mortgage your ship to pay your fines."

"Geez," Floyd muttered to himself. "It didn't cost me this much when they caught me stealing them."

So there he was again—a goof-off and a failure who could screw it up even while winning an automobile.

YOU CAN BE GOOD AND STILL BE MEDIOCRE

Being good at something is no assurance that you'll rise above mediocrity. It depends upon what you're good at. You must want to be good at something that offers you a chance to achieve greatness.

Suppose you drop out of high school and get a job at Charlie's Service Station. Charlie puts you to work on the grease rack. Soon you're giving the best oil-change and lube jobs in town. Charlie is delighted with your work. He pays you the maximum wage for a grease monkey: $4.50 an hour.

So far as quality of life is concerned, being the best grease monkey in town gets you mediocrity at best. If being a grease monkey at $4.50 an hour makes you happy, more power to you. But most adults aren't happy at that level of achievement. To achieve greatness, you have to decide to move on to more rewarding challenges. But if you don't know what you want, you'll remain mired in mediocrity.

That's the situation I found myself in as a Navy ship's storekeeper. I was good at my job. But where was it getting me?

THE SHIP'S STOREKEEPER

Normally, the job of ship's general storekeeper goes to a senior enlisted man. Floyd held the lowest rating of any sailor ever to occupy that position on a cruiser.

Floyd loved his job. He loved the food. And he loved the ship. On the job, he was very conscientious, just as he had been when he was helping his dad on the milk route. For the first four years, he advanced quite rapidly through the enlisted ranks, eventually becoming an E-5—a petty officer second class.

The officers liked the way Floyd performed. They might not have liked **him,** *but they liked his performance, and they rewarded it. Maybe that's why Floyd liked the Navy. When he did a good job, he got recognized for it.*

But it eventually dawned upon him that E-5 was about as high as he was going to go in the Navy. Sure, he could put in his time, behave himself, and maybe rise to first-class, or even chief petty officer. But those were modest goals and they had no glitter for him. He was bumping his head against a ceiling, and he had to decide whether to look for a higher ceiling. A sailor's life is fine for a young lad who wants to sow his wild oats in far-flung places. It's not the ideal life for a man ready to settle down with a family.

YOU MAY HAVE TO SHOP AROUND

Sometimes, it's easier to decide what you **don't want** than it is to decide what you want. You may decide to quit your job at Charlie's Service Station and open a station of your own, with the help of a loan from the Small Business Administration. Then you find that the skills required to run a small business are quite different from the skills required to perform a good lube job.

So you sell the station, pay off the loan, and go into the insurance business. You discover that you've got potential as a salesperson, but you're not sure you want to invest the time necessary to build up a respectable income in the insurance business.

Don't be afraid to change careers more than once if that's what's necessary to find what you want to do. Sometimes deciding what you really want is a process of elimination—like choosing a house to buy. You may not have a clear idea of what you want until you've had a chance to look over several possibilities.

I didn't go directly from Navy enlisted man to successful businessman. I went through some trial and error.

BACK ON THE MILK ROUTE

Floyd left the Navy in 1962 and returned to Detroit. He decided to follow in his dad's footsteps and buy a milk route. He took the cheapest one he could buy—in a rough neighborhood of downtown Detroit. Fifteen percent of his customers were brothels.

Not long after he started the route, he pulled into an alley and prepared to make his deliveries. He was just reaching into the back of the truck when he heard a voice behind him.

"Hey man."

He turned and looked into a couple of black faces. They were calm and non-threatening, except for the knife each one held in his right hand.

"What's up?" Floyd asked, trying to sound cool.

"Hey man, we ain't gonna hurt you. All we want's a little bread to keep us warm and fed. Now you ain't gonna give us no hard time are you?"

"What if I ain't got no bread?"

"Then you ain't got no milk either, sucker. How'd you like to see every one of them bottles busted on the pavement?"

"How much do you want?"

"How much you got?"

They settled on an amount. They were greedy enough, but they didn't want to get into major trouble. And Floyd didn't want to lose everything in his truck.

That started a relationship that was to last for several Saturdays. They knew exactly when Floyd was going to show up in that alley, and they were always there.

One day Floyd was telling his younger brother Ken about it. Ken was 6 feet 5, and he didn't take crap off anybody.

"Why do you let them do it?" he asked.

"Because I don't want to lose my whole inventory," Floyd said. "I pay them a little protection money and they leave me alone."

"Tell you what I'm gonna do," said Ken. "I'm going along with you and see how those cats operate."

"I don't want no trouble, Ken."

"You won't get any. Just let me ride in the back of the truck. I'll be real quiet."

So Ken rode in the back of the truck, and when they reached that alley, the two hoodlums showed up on schedule. Floyd was ready to hand them their regular pay when he heard the clang of that truck door opening. It sounded like the opening of the cell doors of hell. The two hoodlums looked, in fact, as if they had just seen a vision from hell. There stood Ken—all 6 feet 5 inches of him—with a machete in one hand and a rifle in the other.

The robbers froze in their tracks.

Ken's words thawed them out: "Come near my brother again and you're dead."

They turned and ran. Floyd never saw them again.

Ken was a nervy kid, but his luck eventually ran out. He got into heroin, and one sad day he became the victim of murder.

Floyd was going broke fast on the milk route. The trouble was that he was too honest. That may sound a bit strange, considering his earlier years swiping cars, but in truth he was always an honest kid in one sense: He would never lie to you.

When he started that milk route, he handed out price lists to his customers. The other milkmen heard about it and told him he was crazy. You don't let people know the legitimate price for your milk. Most of Floyd's customers were tenants, and they were likely to move out at any time. When they did, most of them didn't bother to pay the milkman. So every week, he was stuck with somebody who didn't pay him. The other milkmen compensated by overcharging the customers who did pay.

It's generally considered to be quite ethical to set your prices high enough to cover any losses from non-payers. But honest Floyd played by the dairy's rules, which didn't take into consideration the different levels of honesty in different types of neighborhood. His milk business was starting to curdle when he received a letter from the Navy inviting him to re-enter the service.

YOUR WANTS MAY BE GREATER THAN YOU THINK

Being a milkman is about like working at a grease rack. Both are honorable jobs and there's nothing wrong with them if that's what you like to do and you're willing to live with the limited income opportunities.

But most of us eventually end up marrying and starting families. We want the best for those families. As a young person, you may think that all you want from life is a steady paycheck, three square meals a day, a comfortable home and a dependable car.

But that doesn't take into account the expenses of rearing and educating kids, paying for orthodontists, enjoying a rich social life and providing quality service to your community.

If you've grown up on the streets of Detroit, absorbing the cultural values of a cat, you may not know that you want these things. Then you meet someone you want to spend the rest of your life with. You know that she deserves nothing but the best. And you know you want to give it to her. Such a person was Linda.

A GIRL NAMED LINDA

Floyd met Linda in 1963. He was 22 years old, and his four-bit '49 Chevrolet had been replaced by a newer Impala. Bill and Floyd had gone to see "West Side Story" at the movie theater and from there they went out on a girl-hunting expedition. They were still empty-handed at midnight, when they pulled up to Wood's Drive-In and Restaurant.

"Let's get something to eat and head home," said Bill.

They gave the curb girl their order, then waited. Floyd pulled out a cigarette.

"Got a match?" he asked. The car's cigarette lighter wasn't working.

"Sorry man," said Bill. "The last one you borrowed cleaned me out."

Floyd glanced at the car next to them. He blew the horn and lowered his window. The person in the next car lowered the window too.

Floyd's glance turned into a double-take. When Webster came up with the word "beauty" he must have had this girl in mind. She had dark hair and brown eyes. If Studebaker had looked as good as she did, it would have outsold Chevrolet.

"Could I borrow a match?" Floyd asked.

"Sure," she said.

"What's your name?" asked Floyd as he lit up.

"Linda Tiracchia." When she said the name, a lyric from "West Side Story" came to mind:

Say it loud and there's music playing;
Say it soft and it's almost like praying.

Floyd would have fought the Sharks and the Jets simultaneously for a chance to see more of her, but this time all he had to do was chain smoke for a few minutes. Four cigarettes and four borrowed matches later, he knew that he had to know her much better. She not only lit his cigarettes; she lit his fire as well.

Bill hitched a ride home with Linda's girlfriend, and Linda and Floyd drove to Chandler Park, a city recreation area. Floyd turned on the radio, they listened to the music, and they talked. They discovered a mutual love for rhythm and blues. And Floyd discovered a love for Linda that was to last a lifetime.

They started going steady immediately. He was still running his milk route and she was a cashier at Lombardi's Food Market. Her father ran a small bar. He earned enough to support a family, but he was no competition for Trader Vic's.

Seven months after Linda lent him that first match, Floyd proposed to her. They were married after a five-month engagement. He couldn't afford a ring.

The wedding may have been noisier than Floyd's first wedding with Nancy Ellsmore in her garage when he was 7 years old. But it wasn't any fancier.

At first they planned to have it in Bill Robertson's basement. In fact, they painted the basement for the occasion. But then Linda's dad decided he would rent Roma Hall in downtown Detroit.

It was the cheapest hall in the roughest neighborhood you could find. Floyd's old gang arrived in leather jackets, bearing an envelope to which each had contributed approximately 50 cents. The entertainment was a juke box.

They spent their wedding night in a motel on Woodward Avenue, then spent two days where all young couples from Detroit go for their honeymoons: Niagara Falls. They returned to Detroit to set up housekeeping in a $65-a-month flat.

Maybe it wasn't a great wedding. But it's been a great marriage.

MARRIAGE IS NOT A MAGIC FORMULA

Marriage is not a magic formula for putting purpose in your life. Many young couples are convinced that they can live indefinitely on love. For some, the honeymoon is a long-running engagement. But eventually, they have to get down to the real work of nurturing and sustaining a marriage and a home.

Money problems can poison a marriage when they're added to all the other problems a young couple faces. That's why it's best for both partners to know what they want to achieve and to have a clear strategy for achieving it.

If they come out of the honeymoon period with no clear knowledge of what they want from life and no clear conception of the price they'll have to pay, they're in for some rocky times.

BACK IN NAVY BLUE

The Wickman marriage had to be made in heaven, or it would not have survived those early years. Floyd's milk business was going sour; he knew his formula for greatness would not come out of a Twin Pines bottle. Yet he had no clear idea of what he wanted beyond the milk route. In his moment of uncertainty, the Navy stepped in with an offer that sounded attractive. It offered Floyd a chance to stay in Detroit and train Navy reservists. It seemed like a good opportunity to him. So aimlessly, he took advantage of the offer and went back into uniform.

True to form, he failed the first test. To train those reserves, he had to go to Instructor Training School. To get into IT school, he had to pass an aptitude test. He flunked it, of course. Nobody ever accused Floyd Wickman of being a woolly-headed scholar.

But he was good at what he did. He had been a storekeeper aboard the Galveston, *so they made him a storekeeper on shore. He was put in charge of the Navy Exchange in addition to his duties around the Navy Reserve armory.*

By this time, life was getting a bit complicated. Not long after their marriage, Linda was pregnant with Floyd Jr. They needed all the money Floyd could make. In addition to handling his Navy duties and running the Navy Exchange, he would also tend bar at his father-in-law's place.

Floyd put in four more years with the Navy, but his attitude started going down hill. He wasn't moving up in rating and there was nothing there to challenge him. He and his detail had to guard the armory, which meant they had to stay up all night. The United States wasn't expecting any invasion from Ontario, and Floyd figured that any problem short of that could wait until morning. So at 10 o'clock he'd go to sleep. On many a morning the chief would come in expecting to find him at his guard desk and instead would hear snores coming from upstairs.

Floyd wasn't very respectful of superior officers. When he responded to an officer it was more likely to be "b--- s---" than "Aye Aye, Sir."

That kind of attitude brought him to a couple of captain's masts and he started getting knocked down in rank. That's why the Navy and Floyd called it quits after nearly 10 years of association. Instead of being afire with enthusiasm, he was burned out. So when his hitch was up, he got out. The year was 1967. He was 25 years old with a wife and two sons, and a third on the way. Outside of his family, he had no accomplishments to boast about, no skills to build upon and no goals to pursue. The situation was pretty well wrapped up in a one-word description: failure.

The years in the Navy had been an improvement of sorts from Floyd's years in the streets. At least he wasn't stealing cars and wasn't doing time.

But he still hadn't latched on to the formula for success.

The military can be a very rewarding career. Many a kid with no money and no education has found career training in one of the armed services. Many a young person has come out with the skills needed to launch a prosperous career. Many have used their re-enlistment bonuses as nest eggs, retired in early middle age, and built satisfying civilian lives with the help of accumulated savings.

But not Floyd Wickman. He entered the Navy with no objective other than to get away from the boredom of Detroit. He re-entered it with no objective other than to find a regular paycheck in the vicinity of Detroit. Without aim and without direction, he ended up where he started: in the lower enlisted ranks.

Admiral Farragut said, "Damn the torpedoes, full speed ahead."

Floyd Wickman said, "Drop the anchor. This looks like a good place to hang out."

YOU CAN'T HANG OUT FOREVER

But you can't hang out forever. At some point, you have to decide what you want in life and start working toward achieving it.

You can't find greatness if you don't know what you're looking for. You have to have a purpose in life—a purpose that will focus your energy and help you achieve what you want to achieve.

If you don't know what you want, your energy will be wasted like the water pouring over a dam. And what you get will be mediocrity.

List the most important points you have gained from the preceding Lesson:

I will speak in front of
2,300
people...

Lesson Four

Greatness Won't Find You; You Have to Go After It

Just knowing what you want will not take you to greatness. You've got to take yourself there.

Walter Russell, a noted artist, sculptor and author, once remarked, "I believe that mediocrity is self-inflicted and that genius is self-bestowed." He might have used the word "greatness" instead of "genius," but I would amend his statement even further. To say that mediocrity is self-inflicted is to imply that you have to do something to yourself to become mediocre. It's been my experience that mediocrity does not result from something you do. It results from all the things you don't do.

My life began to turn around when I discovered that you don't get to greatness by just taking things as they come. You get there by deciding what you want to do, then ***doing*** it. You may wake up in the morning knowing exactly what you want and exactly what you have to do to get it. But unless you're willing to get out of bed and get to work, you'll never be anything better than mediocre. You'll be like the guy I'll call Johnny. His mother was having trouble getting him out of bed.

"C'mon Johnny," she called, "It's time to get up and go to school!"

"I don't wanna go to school," said Johnny.

"But you've gotta go to school," said his mother.

"Give me one good reason why I should get up and go to school," demanded the son.

"I'll give you two," she said. "Number one, you're 47 years old. And number two, you're the principal. Now get up and get to school."

WAKING UP TO ABILITIES

At the age of 25, Floyd Wickman was a long way from being a school principal, but he was a bit like Johnny. He had responsibilities, but there was still a lot of boy in him. He had abilities, but they were still asleep somewhere inside him.

Yet he had to get up and get out into the school of life.

It was his sister Denise who tried to shake him awake.

"Floyd," she said, "You ought to try real estate."

She said that because her husband, Dick, was in real estate and making a pretty good living at it.

Common sense should have told Floyd he would be no good in sales. He was never comfortable when talking to strangers. Even today, when he finds himself among a crowd of people in a social setting, he feels uncomfortable.

STREET SMARTS VS. SOCIAL SKILLS

In a battle of wits, Floyd could hold his own quite well. He had street smarts, which meant that he could talk his way out of a jam if he had to.

But when it came to the social skills required to meet strangers and cultivate friendships—in other words, the skills required to be a good salesperson—Floyd was unlearned and inept.

But since he was unacquainted with all the finer points of selling real estate, he didn't know that he was unqualified. How hard could it be to sell real estate? You sit around the office and wait until a couple comes in saying, "We want to buy a house." You show them a nice house in their price range. They make an offer, the seller accepts and you pocket the commission. Easy money, right?

If you think it's easy, try it for a while. It's a good way to lose weight without exercising. You'll do a lot of sitting, but not much eating.

Floyd spent two months studying for the real estate exam. Eight years in the Navy hadn't made a scholar out of him, but you didn't have to be a genius to pass. All you had to do was score 75 on the test. Floyd scored 75. No more, no less.

He reported for work at the same office where Dick worked. It was in Warren, Michigan, a working-class suburb northeast of Detroit. He was feeling pretty important. It was the first civilian job he'd held that required him to wear a tie.

THERE'S LOTS TO LEARN

There's one thing every prospective real estate agent needs to realize: Passing the real estate exam doesn't mean that you know how to sell real estate. Scoring a 75 on the real estate exam doesn't even mean that you're 75% of the way toward being a salesperson.

There are techniques and principles involved, and it takes effort and attention to learn them. I knew little or nothing about them, and wasn't aware that I needed to learn.

IT TAKES THREE PARTIES

One of the first things you learn as a real estate person is that it takes three parties to bring about a successful transaction. There has to be a buyer. There has to be a seller. And there has to be an agent.

When you go to work in the morning, only one of those parties is present. That's you, the agent. You have to find the other two parties and bring them together. That takes more effort than you might think.

Strangers will not beat a path to your desk begging you to list their houses for sale. Neither will they come to you begging you to sell them a house. Real estate is a competitive business, and the listings and sales go to the agents who know how to find buyers and sellers and provide service to them.

Some salespeople go into real estate with the idea that they can make it just by selling to friends. Within a short time, these people become known as former real estate agents.

My friends were mostly people like me—recent graduates of street gangs, or Navy enlisted personnel whose assets consisted of a skimpy wardrobe of bell-bottoms and Dixie-cup caps plus a couple of six-packs of Stroh's in the refrigerator. Even if they were all flush with money, how many friends do you have who are in the market for a house? And once you've sold each of them a house, whom do you sell next? Buying a house isn't like buying a car. You don't keep it two years, then trade it in.

So I entered the real estate field with no aptitude, no training, no goals, and no confidence. I got into it for about the same reason I got into the Navy: It seemed to be the only convenient option.

It wasn't long before my fellow agents were calling me "the undertaker." It seemed that the only people I ever hauled around to show houses were dead prospects.

THE HIGH DROPOUT RATE

A lot of people go into real estate with the aim of making a fortune. Seventy percent of them become dropouts during their first two years.

Floyd almost joined the crowd.

Oh sure, he sold some houses. There was this young couple coming in looking for a starter home. He showed them a two-bedroom house without a basement. It sold for $8,900. It was in their price range. It was livable. And they bought it. No great sales ability required there.

The problem is that Floyd had only about five of those deals his first 11 months in the business. That netted him, on average, about $80 a week.

YOUR TWO OPTIONS

Everybody who goes into business has two options: success and failure. It's a matter of choice, not luck. If you don't consciously choose success, you gravitate unconsciously toward failure. Remember this famous Wickman saying: Greatness waits for those who go after it. Mediocrity comes to those who stand and wait.

You want mediocrity in the real estate business? I'll tell you how you achieve it. You join the legion of the aimless and you do what most real estate salespeople do. You come into the office at 9 in the morning. You scan through the multi-listings until about 10:30. Then you drive over to see whether your sign is still up on Saginaw Street. Then you go back and cover your three hours of floor time.

THOSE PESKY PHONE CALLS

Floor time is relaxing time. In the real estate business, it means that you're the agent designated to take incoming telephone calls. You write letters to your friends, or read the sports section of the newspaper, or do one of a thousand other things that make absolutely no contribution to your financial well-being.

Every now and then the telephone rings, which is annoying when you're in the middle of a story about the game between the Tigers and the Yankees. You let your annoyance show when you answer it. Who the heck do those callers think they are, interrupting your conversation to inquire about the homes you have for sale?

After floor time, you do your little favors for other salespeople.

"Floyd, can you show a house for me?" asks Pete.

"Sure, Pete."

So you show the house. If the people decide to buy, Pete pockets the commission and Floyd earns nothing but gratitude, which doesn't make car payments.

Pretty soon, it's 9 o'clock at night; you've put in 12 hours and it's time to go home. You'll eat hamburger, if you're lucky, because you haven't earned a dime that day.

That's a typical day in the lives of 70% of the people in real estate—the 70% who get out of the business during the first two years.

STRUGGLING ON $80 A WEEK

That first year was a tough one for Floyd and his family. Macomb County, Michigan, was not a high-income suburb, but it wasn't cheap either. Money went a lot farther in the middle '60s than it does today, but $80 a week was not a princely income for a man trying to support a wife and three kids.

Linda and Floyd learned a lot about handling creditors during that period of their lives. One thing they learned was that you can't squeeze blood out of a rock. The second thing they learned was that if you call your creditors before they call you, they'll work along with you. The third thing they learned is that you don't make promises.

Floyd made that mistake a hundred times. He would say, "I'm working on this sale, and as soon as it closes I'll pay you." As soon as it closed, he would have a dozen other bills clamoring for priority, and the money wouldn't begin to cover them all.

He found that it was much better to say something like, "As soon as it closes, I'll set aside 10% of the commission for you."

Fortunately, Linda's dad knew the situation. He would give the young couple $50 every now and then. And sometimes her folks would come over with a bag of groceries. Floyd's dad couldn't help much; he was still broke.

For one month during that first year, Floyd actually did join the 70% who drop out. He left real estate and tried to get started as an insurance salesman. He soon concluded that this too was the path to starvation. In the insurance business, they talk a lot about the long term: "In 15 years you'll start getting some good royalties." Floyd figured he couldn't go 15 years between meals. So he went back to real estate.

ENTER HITLER'S BROTHER

By this time, management had changed and Floyd went to work for the guy he came to call H.B. The initials stand for Hitler's Brother. He was to change Floyd's life.

H.B. was not one of those guys who greeted each new listing with a rousing chorus of "Hail to the Conquering Heroes." It was more like der fuehrer *dressing down a general who had just overrun most of Europe but couldn't quite take Moscow. It got so bad that the agents would try to sneak their listings through the back door. Otherwise, H.B. would rip through them the way the Blitzkrieg ripped through Poland.*

"J---- C-----, Floyd!" he'd rave. "You can't get $14,000 for that house. You'll get $10,000, maybe $10,500 tops. Get that asking price down about four grand."

"I know it's overpriced, but that's what the sellers insist on. I can't talk them into coming down $4,000."

"Then get them to come down $1,000—four times," H.B. would growl, circling the price with his ballpoint pen. "What's this 90-day listing crap? You know that 40% of the houses take longer than 90 days to sell. You want to do all the spadework, then let somebody else take over the listing?"

"For Pete's sake, H.B., I'm only trying to give the sellers what they want."

"What the sellers want is a sale. You'll not get it this way. And what kind of commission is this you're asking? You know that's below our normal percentage."

"Yeah, but they're a nice couple. Commissions are negotiable, aren't they?"

"Yeah, but you can negotiate your way to bankruptcy. It takes money to run this business, and I've got to get it out of the commissions, unless you want to make up the difference out of your own pocket."

Sometimes, when H.B. got extra picky, he reminded Floyd

of the guy who used to make him run back to the doorsteps and turn the milk bottles so that the Twin Pines Dairy label was facing the street.

One day when H.B. was riding him particularly hard, Floyd got his back up.

"You can't tell me what to do," he said. "I'm an independent contractor."

"Then do your independent contracting somewhere else," he snarled. "We're not going to list properties, spend our lives servicing them, have them expire, then let a co-broker re-list and get the commission."

H.B. SEEMED TO CARE

Despite the fire and bluster that always seemed to surround H.B., Floyd had the feeling that H.B. really cared. Later, he would reflect that H.B.'s concern was strictly with business; Floyd Wickman was just another salesperson. But H.B. wanted Wickman to succeed, because when Wickman succeeded H.B. succeeded too.

There were no fireworks the first time Floyd talked to H.B. The guy could be smooth as silk, and this time he was in a gentle mood.

"Floyd," he said, "You seem like the kind of guy who should be doing good in this business. What do you do all day?"

Floyd gave him a rundown of his daily routine.

"You see, that's the problem," he said. "You don't get any listings that way, and if anybody should be a lister, you should be a lister. What kind of programs are you taking?"

"Programs? What do I need a program for? I passed the real estate exam, so I know the business."

"Yeah, but you've got to go to Dale Carnegie. You've got to learn how to be a salesperson. You don't get to be one just by having a card that says 'Floyd Wickman, Salesperson.' Have you ever heard of STI?"

The Sales Training Institute was unknown to Floyd.

"Well, I'm going to have them call you. And if you can, get into that program."

H.B. had a way of talking to you so that you'd believe anything he said. So when the people from STI called, Floyd enrolled—under orders from H.B. It changed his life.

What Floyd learned from H.B. was quite simple: Achieving greatness requires movement. You don't sit still and wait for greatness to arrive. You go out in search of it. You take courses, you observe the techniques of successful people, and you apply what you've learned.

Until H.B. took him under his wing, Floyd had been a failure as a real estate salesperson. Why? Because he had not gone after greatness.

And why hadn't he gone after greatness?

Because he wasn't aware that it was in him to achieve it. He was Floyd Wickman, former El Duches gang member, former swiper of automobiles, a young man who, during 10 years in the Navy, was able to rise no higher than E-5. H.B. shook him awake, roughly but effectively, and the lessons of the first 26 years of life began to come home to Floyd. Now it remained for him to apply these lessons in following the ***Seven Steps to Achieving Your Full Potential.***

A REVIEW OF THE LESSONS

Here are the lessons I had to apply in order to take the **Seven Steps:**

(1) Early choices don't have to bind you for life.

It's a cliche, but like most cliches it's grounded in truth: You're never too old to change. No matter how rotten your early decisions were and no matter how little you have achieved up to this point, don't give up on yourself. Leave those early choices and your previous failures in the past. You can't change the past, but so what? You're not going to spend the rest of your life in the past. You're going to be living in the future, and it can be shaped by the choices and actions you make from here on.

I learned this lesson by realizing that others who have achieved their full potential had backgrounds that were similar to or worse than mine. Can you feel the joy this one revelation could mean to you? Almost like a toothache going away immediately or shackles being dissolved.

(2) You can't rise to greatness on a bad self-image.

If you don't believe in yourself, who will? If you believe you're a mediocrity, you'll always be a mediocrity. You will never rise above your self-image. So go to work on your self-image. You have everything it takes to achieve greatness: a pair of hands, a pair of legs and a brain. Find something you like to do and can do well. Be as good at it as you can possibly be. Cultivate a supportive circle of friends. As they cheer you on, you will find your self-esteem growing and you'll be ready for greatness. William James, known by many as the father of modern-day psychology, said it best: "The most interesting discovery of my generation is that men can change their life if they change their mind." What that meant to me was, "Oh, gee, all I have to do is start changing how I think about me." I want you to feel the same way that I felt.

(3) If you don't know what you want, mediocrity is what you'll get.

Decide what you want to achieve in life. Be realistic, but aim high. It's better to aim for a star and hit an eagle than to aim for an eagle and hit a rock. An assignment at a training course taught me this. They had a production contest. I decided I wanted to win it, even though the prize was negligible. And I won. This was the first time I ever won anything. It dawned on me that it was because I never had a specific goal to shoot for. Lack of goals kept me in mediocrity.

(4) Greatness won't find you; you have to go after it.

Once you know what you want, find out what you need to do to get it. Then ***do*** it. Here's a self-talk motivational sentence for you. It'll be easy to remember because it only has 10 words, in each word just two letters. But it's the essence of changing your life. The talk is: "If it is to be, it is up to me."

Are you ready to let these lessons sink in? If you are, and when they do, you will be rewarded with the fortitude to follow the journey toward achieving your full potential. To help these lessons sink in, say them out loud to yourself, with enthusiasm, in the first person, several times, and then read on.

List the most important points you have gained from the preceding Lesson:

Part Two

THE SEVEN STEPS TO ACHIEVING YOUR FULL POTENTIAL

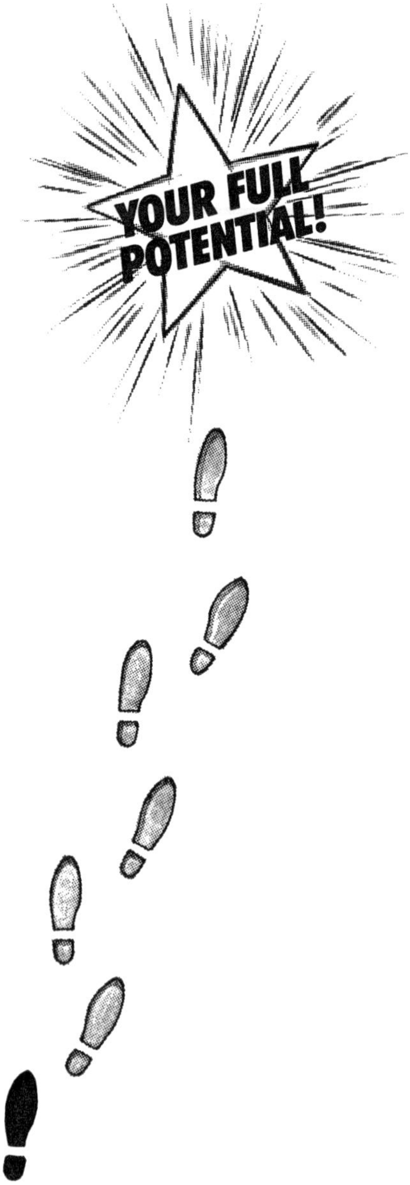
YOUR FULL POTENTIAL!

Step One

Wake Up to Your Capacity for Greatness

It's time now to start taking the **Seven Steps to Achieving Your Full Potential.** The first one isn't hard. All you have to do is become aware of your capacity for greatness. It's there within you. Everyone has the capacity to become great in some pursuit. But until you become aware of this capacity, you won't act on it.

Why is this true?

We adjust our thoughts, our actions and our habits to the environment we think we're in. Suppose you're walking across the desert. You're hot and thirsty. You take a couple of swallows from your canteen. You think how nice it would feel if you could pour the rest of the water over your head and cool off. But you don't, for fear that you might run out of water to drink.

But suppose you knew that just a half-mile ahead was a spring bubbling over with cool drinking water. You'd go ahead and treat yourself to that splash of water from your canteen, knowing that you would be able to replenish it within a few minutes.

You would base your actions on the environment you perceived. If you perceived a desert environment, you would horde your water. If you perceived an oasis environment, you would indulge yourself.

Now write this down somewhere: You're living in an environment full of opportunities for greatness. The universe is a mother lode of treasures for those who are willing to go after them in faith. Indulge yourself. Go for the treasures. Go for greatness.

A lot of people cheat themselves out of rewarding lives because they refuse to open themselves to this awareness. They never rise above mediocrity because they fail to acknowledge a fundamental truth: Each of us harbors the ingredients of success.

So what is your excuse?

Are you ignorant?

That can be fixed.

Are you short on cash?

You don't need a fortune to take the first of the **Seven Steps to Achieving Your Full Potential.** You just need to open your eyes.

Are you too young? If you're young, you're starting out with the greatest treasure you can ask for: time.

Are you too old?

Colonel Sanders was no spring chicken when he started making his millions. It wasn't Little Miss Moses who became the famous painter. It was Grandma Moses.

The truth is, you have no valid excuse for mediocrity. The universe is an environment of plenty. You just have to open your eyes to it.

DON'T BE AFRAID OF IMAGINARY HAZARDS

Sometimes you may cling to an unsatisfactory situation because you're afraid of unseen perils. In your mind's eye, you can see all sorts of dangers lurking in the darkness. In your imagination, you have constructed a dangerous environment and you're acting as if it actually exists. You're like the man who was walking across a railroad trestle at night. It was a long trestle, and before he got to the other side, a speeding locomotive came along.

He knew he couldn't make it to the end of the trestle, and he knew that if he stayed where he was he would end up first cousin to sausage. So to save his life, he dropped between the cross-ties and hung on.

It was a long train, and by the time it had passed, the man was too tired to pull himself back up between the cross-ties. So he just hung there in the black night, dreading the thought of letting go and plunging to his death below.

The night was cold. Each time he moved his fingers, he picked up splinters from the cross-ties. His arms ached with fatigue and muscle strain.

Finally, he could hold on no longer. With a final prayer for the repose of his soul, he turned loose. And dropped two feet into soft sand.

The man's problem was that he had constructed in his mind a false environment. He convinced himself that he was swinging over a rocky gorge. In fact, the soft, sandy ground was just beneath his feet. He could have let go at any time and walked away safely.

In real life, we hang on in unpleasant, unrewarding situations much longer than we need to because we are afraid of what awaits us in the unseen future. Most of the time, the unseen future consists of opportunities just beneath our feet.

YOU WERE NOT BORN TO MEDIOCRITY

Some people seem to be born with unseen weights holding them down. They're like the eagle who thought it was a prairie chicken.

An Indian boy had robbed an eagle's nest and dropped one of the eggs on the way back to his tepee. A prairie hen took the egg under her wings and hatched it along with her own eggs. The eagle grew up with prairie chickens, pecking at grass seeds and worms, flapping its wings and fluttering from knoll to knoll, never rising more than a few feet from the ground. One day it looked up and saw a majestic bird soaring on the rising wind currents.

"Wow! Would I love to soar like that," said the eagle.

"Forget it," said a prairie chicken. "That's an eagle. You're a prairie chicken. Prairie chickens don't fly that far off the ground."

And so the young bird grew into an old bird, thinking it was an earth-bound prairie chicken, never realizing that it was an eagle born to reach for the sky.

Many people deny themselves the rich rewards of greatness because they think they were born to mediocrity and are incapable of rising above it. They are wrong. They have wings to soar on, if they'll just become aware of them and spread them.

DON'T LET OLD FRUSTRATIONS HOLD YOU BACK

Some people have allowed past frustrations to condition them to mediocrity. They allow these frustrations to defeat them long after the cause of the frustration has passed. They're like the elephant I used to visit at the Detroit Zoo. It was a listless monster that seemed to have no initiative. It just stood in the middle of its pen, not moving toward the water when it was thirsty; not moving toward the hay when it was hungry.

A zookeeper told me the story.

When it was young, that elephant was full of energy. In fact, it was so energetic that the zoo management feared it would damage something or somebody by accident. So the elephant's keepers started a program of conditioning.

First, they drove a heavy steel stake, about 8 feet long, into the ground. A chain was fastened to the stake and tied around the elephant's leg. When the elephant ran with its customary energy, the chain would go taut and it would cut into its leg. Eventually, the metal stake was replaced with a wooden one, and the chain was replaced by a rope. The elephant could have broken the rope or the stake any time it wanted, but by now it was conditioned. The expectation of pain was enough to keep it docile.

By the time I knew the elephant, the stake had been removed. All that was left was a piece of rope tied around its leg. The elephant was free to move anywhere it wanted. But the animal didn't know it. In its awareness, the heavy chain and the steel stake were still there to inflict pain if the big animal exceeded permissible limits.

Studies show that 60% to 80% of the people in the American work force are unhappy with their jobs. In fact, 40% of them hate their jobs. They could move on. There's nothing really restraining them, except an imaginary chain and stake.

So why do they stay?

For the same reason the eagle didn't try to fly: They think they weren't cut out for anything better. For the same reason the elephant didn't run to its water: They imagine that there are restraints that will cause pain if they stray too far from the familiar. For the same reason the man on the trestle kept hanging on: They imagine dangers that don't exist, and then act as if those dangers were real. They've cultivated habits to fit the environment that they see around them. Awareness shows them a different environment—the true environment. When they become aware of that different environment, they can adjust their behavior accordingly.

That happened to me on the streets of Detroit. My world consisted of street gangs, petty thievery and aimless partying. Work was something you did to stay alive. There were no opportunities for wealth in this environment.

It happened to me in the Navy. The environment there was the enlisted ranks. It never occurred to me that there were routes to a commission, to a position of command, to prestige and privileges.

It almost happened to me in the real estate business. I hung in there with the crowd of non-achievers. That was my environment. I did what they did, because that's what you did in the environment I perceived.

But the opportunities were there all the time.

YOU HAVE A CHOICE

I'm reminded of the two men on an airplane. When the plane achieved cruising altitude and the captain turned off the seatbelt signs, the flight attendant came by and asked, "Can I get you a drink?"

"Yeah," said the first guy. "I'll have a Scotch on the rocks."

The other guy gave her a self-righteous look.

"Ma'am," he said, "I'd rather commit adultery than drink alcohol."

"Jeez," said the first guy. "I didn't know I had a choice."

Well, you have a choice.

When you're young, perhaps you need a job, and so you take the first opportunity. When you get that first job, you're happy to get up, get dressed, hang in there from 9 to 5, then come home to supper, a couple of hours of prime-time television, the nightly news and bed. You're off the streets, you have a roof over your head and you're eating three square meals a day.

Four or five years later, you're into the routine. It's familiar and comfortable. You encounter opportunities to turn loose and go elsewhere, but you scarcely give them a thought. Turning loose means taking a chance. Who knows how far you might fall? Who knows what kind of rocks lie beneath you? You weren't intended for greatness. If you stray too far from your familiar routine, you may feel some pain. That kind of thinking is failure thinking.

ADDICTED TO MEDIOCRITY

In a sense, it's like taking up smoking. It takes a while to get used to contaminating your lungs with tar and infusing your blood with nicotine. You do it because it makes you feel grown-up or cool or sophisticated. In time, smoking becomes a pleasurable experience; you light up because you enjoy it. The morning cough comes later, and you realize that sticking with the habit could jeopardize your health. But by now you're addicted to it. You don't want to stop. You're comfortable with the habit, even though it may inhibit your physical abilities and lead you to an early grave. People get addicted to mediocrity too.

THREE BEDROOMS, ONE BATH AND NO VISION

Jane and Tommy are a typical suburban couple who have become addicted to mediocrity. He's a carpenter and she does secretarial work. Their combined wages enable them to own a three-bedroom, one-bath tract house on a small lot.

They'd both like to move up to a four-bedroom, 2½-bath colonial with a large yard and a swimming pool. But their present situations won't allow it.

Tommy looks around at his environment. He's a good carpenter for a prosperous contractor, but he's already gone about as far as he can go. He can drive nails with the best of them, and whether it's framing a house or putting together a cabinet, nobody can do a better job. But he's reached the top of the scale, and when payday comes around, $12 an hour is the most he can expect.

Jane knows how to type letters and do filing chores. These are mechanical tasks that almost anyone can be taught to perform. But her interests lie outside the office routine. She has an excellent eye for color and style, as anyone can tell from the way she dresses and decorates her home. She is an excellent seamstress who can whip out an eye-catching outfit without benefit of patterns.

What keeps Tommy from taking a few night courses in business management, taking out a building loan, hiring a crew of his own and becoming a home-builder instead of a carpenter?

What keeps Jane from opening a fashion business of her own, either as a retailer or as a designer?

Both are hard workers, but their hard work is wasted. They're exerting themselves in unproductive ways. They could be working hard on things that could lead them to the big colonial home and the in-ground pool. But they haven't looked at the possibilities. They're not even aware that they're out there.

We often look at successful people and think, "Boy, I'd sure like to be who they are."

Who they are has nothing to do with it. It's what they do that counts, and what they do is nothing that you can't do. You need to become aware of that.

If Tommy and Jane only knew it, success is out there waiting for them. I know, because I can cite you the true story of a Virginia couple I'll call Jason and Maxine.

Jason was worse off than Tommy. He had grown up in a rural area of Virginia and had not gone to school. He couldn't read or write. But he could hammer and nail.

Jason took a job nailing on roofing for a contractor who built custom homes for upscale suburbanites. He earned the minimum wage. It wasn't enough to support a family, so his wife, Maxine, would join him on the roof. It was a hard life. Then Jason and Maxine looked up and saw opportunities.

It occurred to Jason that he was going to get nowhere driving nails into roofing. So he began to look around the work site, observing what other people were doing. He learned how to frame a house and how to do a lot of the fancy interior work.

Jason couldn't read or write, but he learned all about building houses. He also learned to figure.

Eventually, Jason decided to strike out on his own. He got a building loan, built a house and sold it. Then he reinvested the profit in other houses. Soon people were coming to him asking him to build their custom homes.

Jason and Maxine moved out of their rented home into a fine house that Jason built in one of those upscale neighborhoods. Soon they also owned a farm on Virginia's Eastern Shore. Jason would still get in there and work with his crews. Sometimes Maxine would too. They were still driving nails, but they were also driving Cadillacs.

AWARENESS: AN OPENING TO SUCCESS

Jason and Maxine started with awareness. Awareness is more than knowing that something is possible. It's an opening of yourself to the possibilities. It creates a true focus. To best illustrate focus: Did you ever buy a new car? Remember the day you got it. How many did you see on the highway that day? Oh yeah. All of a sudden it seems that everybody else got theirs today too. Actually, they've had their cars for awhile, but now that you're focused on that car, you see them all around you.

In the same way, your awareness allows you to see opportunities that were there all along but that you hadn't noticed because nothing focused your attention on them. Your awareness can start with the realization that "I want something better." In the case of Jane and Tommy, that "something better" can be the four-bedroom colonial with the swimming pool. They can't get it on the wages of a carpenter and a secretary. But they can get it by opening themselves to new possibilities; by becoming aware of a new environment.

AWARENESS DAWNS

Every time Floyd Wickman has grown personally or professionally, the growth has started with this awareness.

Once you become aware of the possibilities, you become a student of everybody and everything.

With a little prodding from H.B., Floyd came to the realization that there was more to selling real estate than coming to work and waiting for prospects to show up. He needed to be taught. So he went to the Sales Training Institute to learn.

You had to take a test to qualify, but that was no big barrier. Floyd knows now that the test was just a sales technique. It increased the perceived value of the course, which was an important objective. The price was $1,100 for a program that consisted of three months of classroom work and six months of correspondence.

Floyd and Linda were flat broke, but he was more afraid of H.B.'s wrath than he was of being broke. So he scraped up the $1,100, passed the test and went to school.

Jim Dow and Matt King were the instructors for that course. There was nothing magical or extraordinary about what they taught. If there were, STI would still be in business. Neither instructor will be remembered as one of the educational greats of our century. But when the student's ready, the teacher appears, and in this case the student was ready.

They read the class a poem. Floyd remembers it this way:

Figure it out for yourself, my lad;
You've all that the greatest of men have had;
Two arms, Two legs, and a brain to use—
A brain to use if only you choose.

That was the first time it dawned on Floyd that he could accomplish anything he wanted. He was 11 months into his first year in real estate before he realized that he didn't have to be a paycheck slave all his life. He could soar to greatness.

What caused this realization?

It wasn't that he was hearing all this for the first time. You read it every time you buy a self-help book. You hear it every time you listen to a speech by a self-made person. You hear it over and over on motivational tapes.

Floyd heard this invigorating truth, but he didn't become aware of it until the moment arrived when he was sitting in the STI session listening to that simple little poem.

Was it because he had finally reached a certain level of maturity—the inevitable process of growing older?

Not likely. If that were true, Floyd wouldn't be meeting so many people now in their 30s, 40s, 50s and 60s who are still looking for success.

Sometimes you don't hear something until it's repeated for the seventh or eighth time. On that particular day, Floyd heard it and believed. And because he believed, things happened.

AWARENESS LEADS TO LEARNING

Why is awareness so important?

Nido Qubein, my North Carolina colleague, makes an important point in his book, Professional Selling Techniques:

> "What you don't know about selling, about your company, about your products and services, and what you don't know about your industry can cost you plenty. But there's a positive side to that: What you do know can help you sell! Brainpower, properly directed, becomes selling power. . . . That is why the professional seeks to learn everything possible and to become the company field expert out in the territory."

So Floyd set out to know what he needed to know about selling. After he became aware of the possibilities for him in real estate, he would never miss a seminar. If there was a meeting that promised new information on success in real estate, he was there. He never saw a book on success in sales or real estate that he didn't buy. If there was an audio recording that would provide him with motivation and pointers, he bought it.

Once you open yourself to awareness, these things jump out at you, as if some unseen hand were directing you toward them.

When you realize that you can succeed, and you make that decision to succeed, you naturally become a student.

THE WOODWORKING CHALLENGE

After Floyd had become a busy and prosperous executive, he decided to take up a hobby. He settled on woodworking. Floyd had never before done anything with his hands. But here he was, turning 40 and slipping into a routine of business during the day, watching the tube at night.

Finally Linda said, "Gee, honey; All you ever do is watch television and spend time with me. Why don't you look around for a hobby?"

It sounded good to Floyd. He needed something apart from his business to relax his mind and recharge his creativity.

He was reading an article on choosing careers in Success *magazine. If you want to find a career, it said, think of what it is you like to do. Floyd thought this would probably work not just for careers but for hobbies too.*

He thought about it. What he liked to do was visit office-supply stores and hardware stores. But office-supply is too much like business.

So what did Floyd like about hardware stores?

Tools. He thought it was neat, all the things you could do with them.

But up to this point he had never made anything with his hands; never fixed anything in his life. When they bought the kids toys for Christmas, Linda was the one who put them together. Floyd didn't know how to do any of that stuff.

Yet, the idea of working with tools appealed to him. So his mind gravitated toward woodworking. It was always amazing to him to look at a beautiful piece of woodwork and say, "Gee. That used to be a tree, and now look at it."

But he didn't know the first thing about transforming a piece of lumber into a thing of beauty. So he went to Sears and ran into a salesperson named Len.

Floyd picked up a tool.

"What's that?" he asked.

"That's a sander."

"No kidding. What does it do?"

"You use it to smooth off rough surfaces and get them ready for stain or varnish or paint."

"Okay, I'll take it. What's this number?"

"It's a jigsaw."

"Is that what they make those puzzles with?"

"It's good for cutting in patterns. You don't have to saw in a straight line."

"Okay. I'll take one."

Floyd bought every woodworking tool Sears had. He partitioned off his basement and lined all those tools up on the walls. He didn't know zip about woodworking, but he was aware that he could learn. He made it his goal to learn, and he committed himself to the task. He still doesn't know everything there is to know about it, but he's making things he never thought he'd be able to make.

Now, Floyd didn't start out by saying, "Hmmmm, I want to be a woodworker. So I'm going to start with Step

A, then proceed to Step B and on through Steps C, D and E."

He started with an awareness of the possibilities in him as a woodworker. He opened himself to this awareness, and the things he needed to become a woodworker came to him. He found the tools, the books, and the advice he needed. He acted upon these and acquired the experience and the skills.

KEEPING TRIM THROUGH AWARENESS

You can follow the same course in doing just about anything you want to do.

For instance, when Linda approached middle age she developed a deep interest in health. She was a sharp looking lady when I met her, and she was determined to keep those sharp looks. So she became a student of good health.

You may remember that we met over cigarettes. I needed a match, and she lit my fire.

Well, Linda decided that smoking was a bad habit to carry into middle age. So she gave it up. Then she started working out in little ways. She started paying attention to her eating habits. The efforts paid off. Even in her late 40s, Linda is a shapely lady. She didn't get there by adopting a systematic course of study. She got there by opening herself to awareness.

Every time there's a television program that has anything to do with health or working out, Linda watches it. She has books all over the house telling her how to stay fit.

She never consciously says, "I'm going to go to the bookstore and buy a book on fitness."

But when new books come out, she's there waiting for them. Books on fitness have always been coming out, but Linda didn't notice them until this fitness awareness came upon her.

So when awareness hits you, you start seeing things for the first time. All of a sudden, when the flyers come out advertising seminars on the topic that interests you, you see them for the first time.

It's as if your subconscious mind has finally got the message: Hey, this person's interested in fitness, or woodworking, or real estate, or fashion design. Armed with this awareness, your subconscious maneuvers you into position to take advantage of all the information that's out there.

AWARENESS BRINGS CONFIDENCE

With this awareness comes the confidence that you will succeed.

Nido Qubein is one of the most successful individuals I know. He is a past president of the National Speakers Association and, like me, has received the organization's top public-speaking award. When people who know him think of Nido, they think of the young Lebanese kid who arrived in the States with $50 in his pocket and not a word of English in his vocabulary. Nido has made a fortune as an author, businessman, professional speaker and management consultant. But that's not why I respect him.

I respect him because he's one of the greatest salesmen I've ever met.

Now I'm no slouch as a salesman myself, and I've met other great salesmen in my life. But I've seen few as complete as Nido.

What makes him a good salesman?

The minute he walks up to you, his mind says, "Now what can I sell this guy?" Nido is always aware of the possibilities, and always ready to make the most of them.

When the awareness hits you—when you perceive that different environment that has always been there—you begin adapting to that new environment in subtle and not-so-subtle ways.

MORE ENERGY, MORE FOCUS ON LEARNING

When Floyd became aware that he had the same equipment all great achievers have—two arms, two legs and a brain—he began to tackle his job more energetically.

It wasn't that he hadn't put in long hours before. He had. But they were unfocused, non-productive hours. Now he stopped following the losing crowd—that 70% of new real estate agents who were headed out of the business.

He began picking up on some of the basics that distinguish the winners from the losers. He became a student of everyone. As a result, he started getting sharper. Every time he went to a seminar or read a book or watched a movie, or listened to an LP album (that was before the days of audiocassettes) concerning sales or success principles, he was hearing it for the first time. Not only was he hearing it; he was also applying it. So everything got better.

Basically, Floyd cultivated good habits. These were habits that were consistent with the new environment of success that he was now aware of.

Until then, he had cultivated "paycheck habits." He had adjusted his lifestyle to the size of his paycheck instead of looking for ways to increase his paycheck.

THE HABITS OF SUCCESS

I learned that in the sales profession there are people who make a habit of earning lots of money. Through boom years and recession years, they sustain those high earnings. How do they do it?

A friend of mine named Dan was one of those people. Dan had been earning $50,000 to $60,000 a year before going into real estate during the '70s. Remember, this was before the era of stagflation that hit during the Carter presidency, so those were 60,000 healthy dollars.

When he got into real estate, Dan continued to pump out those high earnings. Then came 1979 and 1980, when the bottom fell out of the real estate market. During those years, a lot of real estate agents got out of the business, or adjusted their lifestyles to match their lower earnings.

Not Dan. He kept his earnings at the $60,000-a-year level, even during the recession.

He didn't have a secret formula. All he had was a set of good habits. These were habits cultivated through an awareness that success was out there; all Dan had to do was reach for it. And Dan reached. He didn't just go to work in the morning, make the required number of telephone calls, then open up the sports pages. He made the extra calls. He wasn't content with lackadaisical presentations. He developed good presentations and gave them one after another. He looked for and used the sound techniques to bring prospects to the point of a decision.

Dan knew that, even in recession times, people still buy homes. Where other salespeople perceived an endless sales desert, Dan would locate the oasis. He did what was necessary to turn prospective buyers into customers of his.

MASTERING THE BASICS

When an athletic team goes into a slump, the coach or manager usually knows what to do: The team goes back to the basics.

The problem with most non-achievers is that they don't master the basics.

When Floyd Wickman got into real estate, he knew nothing about the basics. He didn't even know there were any basics to learn. He got into it mostly because it looked like easy work.

When he tended bar for his father-in-law, he used to see guys come in during the late afternoon and buy drinks. He figured they must have good jobs or they wouldn't be off so early. And he figured their jobs paid well or they wouldn't be able to buy drinks. He found out that they were real estate agents. So when Dick offered him a chance to get into the business, he saw it as a chance to get off early and have a few drinks.

H.B. tried to teach Floyd some of the basics, but it wasn't until his experience with awareness that the lessons began to sink in.

Floyd can't give you the basics of accounting, engineering or brain surgery, because those aren't his fields. He's an authority on sales, sales management, running a business and cultivating a marriage, because he's been successful in all of those endeavors.

But regardless of your field of endeavor, you can master the basics once you achieve awareness.

SOME BASICS IN THE SALES INDUSTRY

Let's use selling as an example of how you master the basics. One of the fundamentals I learned is that you have to get new business. But you don't get a lot of business by calling all your friends and relatives and saying "Wanna buy a widget?"

You can start with them, but if you're serious about making a living in this field, you don't stop with them. You'll find prospects all over, but first you have to look.

A Boston Irish kid named Mike O'Riley would have made a good salesperson. Mike went to confession one day and told the priest, "Father, forgive me, for I have committed hanky panky."

The good father was a conscientious priest, interested in keeping a clean congregation, so he said to the lad, "Mike, if you expect me to absolve you, you'll have to tell me who it was."

"Oh no, I can't do that, Father," said Mike. "I promised I wouldn't tell."

The priest tried to help him.

"Well, was it Mary at the bakery?"

"No, Father."

"Was it Suzy at the library?"

"Oh, heavens no, Father."

"Was it Veronica at the drugstore?"

"No, father, it was none of the above."

The priest finally sent Mike away, still scarlet with sin, with instructions to be back in two weeks.

As Mike walked out of the church, he encountered his friend, Sean.

"Hey, did you get absolved?"

"No," said Mike, "but I got two weeks off and three good leads."

THE TELEPHONE IS YOUR ALLY

I learned that successful salespeople get good leads by turning the telephone into an ally. To emulate them, you get hold of a city directory, which has telephone numbers and street addresses cross-indexed. Then you start calling.

For real estate agents, assuming that you spend three minutes with each person you reach, you'll contact 20 people an hour. Somewhere in that mass of numbers is a home-owner who's thinking about selling. Another home goes into your inventory of listings.

If you watch successful agents, you'll see them searching through the multi-listings book looking for expired listings. They'll find out why the home didn't sell. Then they'll go to work helping the owner list the property so that it ***will*** sell.

You'll also see them searching out "for sale by owner" ads.

Smart agents know that 70% of these would-be sellers eventually list through agents. So your chances of picking up a listing among these prospects can be as high as 7 out of 10. Not bad odds.

DON'T SPIN YOUR WHEELS

All these things began to sink in once I had convinced myself that success was imminent.

A real estate agent can put in an awful lot of hours doing nothing but wheel-spinning.

The handsome young couple walks in and wants to look at some property in Platinum Park.

You pile them into your Park Avenue and drive them out there. You take them to the four-bedroom contemporary, a symphony of redwood and stone, and you tell them, "This is you."

The "ooohs" and "aaahs" tell you that you're right. She goes for the Cuisinart kitchen. The basement rec room is up his alley. The stone fireplace and the vaulted ceiling with skylight have them both dreaming of cozy fires and bearskin rugs. The large master bedroom with the adjoining bath (sunken Jacuzzi, of course) has them ready for the plunge. She loves the huge walk-in closets and the marble-topped dressing table. He loves the separate dressing rooms. Now he can shave while she puts on her make-up.

There's only one hitch. This is Tommy and Jane. He's still a carpenter and she's still a secretary, and all they can afford is a three-bedroom, one-bath tract house with aluminum siding. They're not shopping, they're dreaming. And they're dreaming on your time.

H.B. tried to tell me about these people. Before you invest your time, qualify them. Make sure they can afford what you're trying to sell. Separate the lookers from the buyers.

Another time-waster is the overpriced property. You've wasted your time picking up a listing if it's priced 15% above its fair market value. And you're wasting your time showing it, even if the prospects can afford the price.

These are the basic facts of life in real estate, and knowing them is what puts the commissions in your pocket. I didn't pick them up through systematic study. I learned them by becoming a student of everything and everybody in the business.

BE AWARE OF TIME

There are basics in your business, too. Regardless of what we do, we need to make efficient use of our time.

All of us can benefit from a time log. Keep a record of everything you do during the day. After a few days, look back over the things you did that contributed nothing to your productivity or profitability. Then find ways of eliminating these things from your work day.

In every business, you'll find people who will waste your time. Find ways to avoid them. One way is to set a specific time of day when you will accept calls or visitors. At other times, have your secretary take calls for you to return. If you know a person tends to take a lot of time on the telephone, wait until a few minutes before lunch or a few minutes before five to call. The person will be eager to get away and won't waste so much time.

At the beginning of each day, make a list of things you need to do that day. Put them in the order of priority. Then tackle them one at a time. If it's a task that can't be completed in one day, break it into smaller sub-tasks.

Finish what you start. Successful people are those who decide what they want to do, then keep at the task until it's finished. Every minute invested in a task that's never finished is a minute wasted.

Spend the most time with the people most likely to contribute to your profitability. The 80/20 rule is a good one to apply. In most businesses, 80% of the profit comes from 20% of the customers. So you should chose the 20% of your prospects who are likely to yield 80% of your profits. Then spend 80% of your time with them.

Watch the successful people in your business. Become a student of them. You'll begin to put together the knowledge and awareness that will lead you on to success.

SUCCESS STARTS IN YOUR MIND

Remember that success starts in your mind. You will never achieve success until your mind is convinced that you are a successful person. The awareness has to be there.

Napoleon Hill, in his book, Think and Grow Rich, tells us that "What the mind can conceive and believe, it can achieve."

William James, the father of modern psychology, said, "One of the most interesting discoveries of my generation is that people can control their activities by changing their minds, and they can change their minds."

The truth of this has been demonstrated repeatedly.

Actually, you have two minds. One is your conscious mind—the one you use to think and reason. It's the one Rene Descartes had in mind when he said, "I think, therefore I am."

The other is the subconscious mind. It's the one you're usually unaware of. It keeps your heart beating, your lungs pumping, and your other organs functioning. It keeps you balanced on your feet, and it regulates your body temperature. It also is the storehouse of memory. You don't keep Aunt Bertha's telephone number constantly in mind. You keep it tucked away in a handy corner of your subconscious until you need it. Then you ask your subconscious to produce it, and presto! Your subconscious flashes it into your conscious mind the way a computer flashes data onto its video screen.

ATTITUDES AND HABITS

Your subconscious is also the storehouse of your attitudes and habits. They've been programmed into it constantly since you were born. Your subconscious believes what your conscious mind tells it, and it will make its subconscious decisions on the basis of that information.

If your conscious mind has been telling your subconscious mind all your life that you're a failure, your subconscious believes what it's told. It therefore saddles you with the attitude of failure and you become a failure in fact.

If your conscious mind has been telling your subconscious that you're a successful person, your subconscious believes it and responds with confident attitudes. You therefore become successful.

SHINING A POSITIVE LIGHT

In Floyd's work training salespeople, he tries to turn on a positive light in the subconscious. He teaches people sales skills through his Floyd Wickman Course®. After a couple of weeks of watching his students, whom he endearingly refers to as his "Sweathogs," he will single out one individual who seems to be saddled with a negative self-image. (Now the Floyd Wickman Course—Sweathogs® is a commonly recognized name in the sales-training industry.) He'll take that person aside and say, "Hey Joan. I have this feeling that you are going to be a top producer."

Joan will look at him with a "Who, me?" expression. She can't believe the instructor would take the time to seek her out individually and tell her she is destined for success. She knows she's facing failure. Floyd knows she's facing failure.

But guess what: Once she gets this positive picture of herself, she becomes successful. A positive mental picture leads to a positive attitude, which leads to success.

It isn't hard to see how the young Floyd Wickman developed the attitude of a loser. There was his dad, constantly telling him that nothing he did was right. Floyd's conscious mind took in that information and passed it on to his subconscious. His subconscious believed it. He became convinced that he could do nothing right. Therefore, he acted like a failure, and so became a failure. He drifted without trying to plot a direction. He let the environment control him.

The moment of awareness in the STI course came when his conscious mind took in the information that he could succeed and passed it on to his subconscious.

It was as if a light bulb had been turned on in Floyd's subconscious. Suddenly he was aware of a new kind of terrain. He wasn't destined to spend his life being a slave to a paycheck. He wasn't swinging from the cross-ties over a deep, rocky chasm. He wasn't tethered to an immovable stake that limited his movements. He could see greatness in himself. He wasn't a grounded prairie chicken. He was an eagle. He could fly!

SHAKE YOURSELF AWAKE

If you've been puttering along in the belief that you're not cut out for success, it's time to shake yourself awake. Look beyond the mediocrity in your immediate environment and start taking in the possibilities for greatness that lie all around you—and that are always present within you.

Once you perceive the opportunities for success, you will begin to cultivate the habits and practices that fit in with a successful environment. You will learn the basics. You will sharpen your abilities. You will focus your efforts, and you will be on your way to success.

Don't be like the man on the trestle, worrying about dangers that probably aren't there. Don't be like the eagle, believing you were born to mediocrity when you have all the equipment you need to soar to greatness. Don't be like the elephant, letting yourself be restrained by a rope that exists only in your imagination. The dangers in front of you are no greater than those successful people have mastered. Mediocrity is your lot only if you let it be. The pain of breaking away from mediocrity isn't nearly as great as the pain of enduring it. Become aware of this and you're ready to continue on the **Seven Steps to Achieving Your Full Potential.**

List the most important points you have gained from the preceding Step:

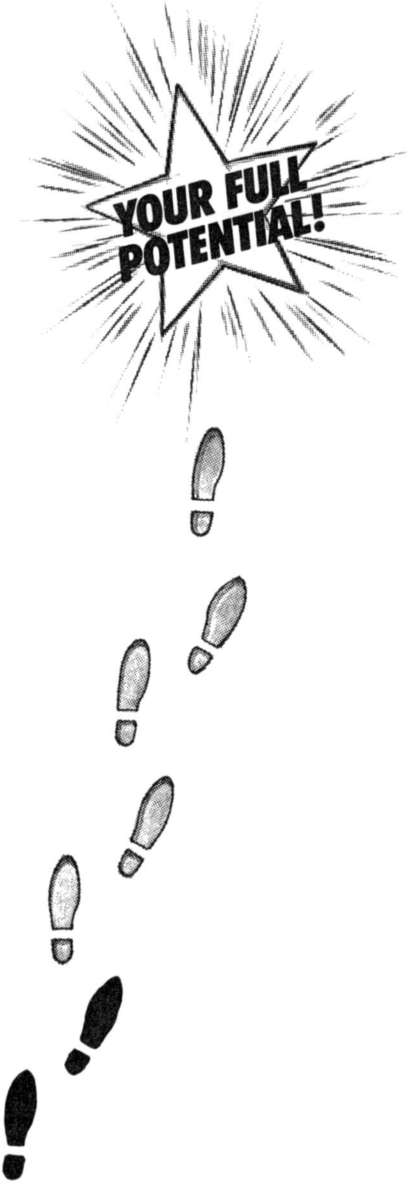
YOUR FULL POTENTIAL!

Step Two

Establish Your Goals—Great Ones and Small Ones

If you want to succeed, set a goal. That's Step Two on the road to greatness.

If you set a goal, you've got the ingredients for success. You'll be on the path toward greatness. It will be like walking through two lines of people who are hitting you on the shoulder and hitting you on the back at the same time. They'll keep pushing you forward. Today I'm a fanatic on goals. Everything I've got, I got because I set a goal.

GOALS PUT YOU IN CONTROL

There's nothing mystical or miraculous about goals. They're not magic formulas. They just give you a focus for positive thinking.

And through positive thinking, you can put yourself in control of your life. Without goals, you're like a ship that puts to sea with no one at the helm. It's out of control. If the destination is England, it may wind up on the coast of Africa, or it may sail in circles around the Atlantic. But when the helmsman takes the wheel and sets a course, it's under control. It's going to reach its destination.

Goals set the course for your life and put you in control. And the only way you can succeed is to be in control. When you're in control, you don't let the clock and the calendar control you. You control your time. You work at high-priority activities—the ones that spell profit for you.

THE CREW MEMBER WITH NO PURPOSE

During World War II, it was discovered that one B-17 crew member was usually more stressed out than anybody else aboard.

It wasn't the pilot. He had a job to do—fly the plane to its target and back, avoid the flak from enemy ground fire, try to keep away from enemy fighters and, if fighters did pounce, put the bomber in position to defend itself with its own guns.

It wasn't the navigator. He had to focus all his attention on the goal of guiding the plane to its target, then back to its home base.

It wasn't the bombardier. He had to focus his mind on a very specific goal. He had to take over the direction of the aircraft for the last few moments before the dropping of the lethal load. It was his job to put the bombs on their target.

It wasn't the gunners. They had to keep their guns in working order, stay alert for enemy fighters, and try to bring them down should they attack.

Each of these men had a specific task, and each was in control of his mission.

The stressed-out bundle of nerves was the one person on board who did not have a goal of his own and who was not in control: the copilot. His role was to sit quietly and be ready to fly the airplane in case the pilot got shot.

If you want to achieve greatness, put yourself in control by adopting a goal and working toward it. In every transaction that goes down, somebody's going to be in control. The winner is the person who decides, "It's going to be me."

If you asked 30,000 of our Sweathogs® whether they were more successful after taking our course than they were before, 29,200 would say "Yes." And if you asked why, the most likely answer would be, "Because I'm in control." In our Floyd Wickman Course—Sweathogs®, that's the number one thing we teach: Be in control of yourself, your time, your attitude, your prospects and your peers.

So I started succeeding when I first set goals and began taking control of my life. Until then, I was like the airline pilot who told his passengers over the intercom: "Ladies and gentlemen, I have good news and bad news. The bad news is that we've lost our course and we don't know where we're going. The good news is that we're making awfully good time."

THE MILLION-DOLLAR GOAL

Floyd called Linda from his office.

"Don't bother to cook, Honey," he said. "Just fix something for the kids and call the sitter. We're going out."

"You must have closed a big one," she said.

"Not yet. But I'm going to."

Floyd took her to a pizzeria on Van Dyke near Lynch Road. It was no gourmet palace. There was no maitre d' in a tux, no linen napkins, and the table cloth was checkered vinyl.

But so far as Floyd is concerned, Linda provides the elegance wherever she goes, so this place was elegant.

He ordered a bottle of wine—cheap stuff, but it was red and Floyd noticed how it set off Linda's dark hair and deep brown eyes.

"So what's the occasion?" she asked after the waiter had delivered their food.

"Linda," said Floyd, "I just decided to go to the top in the real estate business. I'm going to go to the top with or without you. I'd much rather go with you, and I promise you this: When I start succeeding, I'm going to love you as much as or more than I always have. I'm going to give you the things you want. And any day that you think I'm working too much, I'll quit."

That was quite a speech for Floyd. He had never before had the guts to say that to her. As with most things he'd done, he'd made a botch of his marriage during the first couple of years. But now he was committed to making a success of it as well as of himself, and he wanted Linda to buy in to the commitment.

GOALS MADE IT POSSIBLE

Floyd couldn't have made that commitment unless he had set some solid goals and unless he had put confidence in their achievement.

Up to that point, Linda had little reason to put confidence in Floyd. He had tried a number of things—the Navy, a milk route, bar tending and real estate—without making much headway. When the bills came in faster than the paychecks, he would say, "I'm going to try this a little longer."

When you say "I'm going to try," you're giving yourself an excuse for failure: "Gee, Honey, I tried, but it just didn't work out."

This time he didn't say he would try. He said he would go to the top. And he did.

SUCCESS WAS IN THE CARDS

After his moment of truth at that STI course, Floyd went back to his office and took out one of the business cards the company kept for new agents. Each card had printed on it the name, address and telephone number of the business. There was a blank place in which to type the new agent's name.

So Floyd took one of those cards and typed in the blank space, "Floyd Wickman, Million Dollar Club member." He pinned it to the front of his desk.

That was a pretty audacious thing to do. He was announcing to one and all that Floyd Wickman, who hadn't sold diddly during the past 11 months, was going to sell a million dollars' worth of real estate in 1967.

WHEN A MILLION DOLLARS WAS REAL MONEY

Today, making the Million Dollar Club is a nice achievement, but it's not the accomplishment it was back then. In 1967, for an unproductive, semi-starving agent in a working-class suburb of Detroit, making the Million-Dollar Club made the climb to Mount Everest look like a Sunday stroll along the beach.

These days, I like to kid those agents in Southern California, where a modest neighborhood is one in which the houses sell for under $5 million.

"Some of you guys walk around like peacocks with your Million Dollar Club plaques when your average sale price is $2.5 million," I tell them. "What did you do, sell half a house last year?"

In 1967, the average suburban home in Macomb County, Michigan, sold for $11,400. They bring a good deal more today, but they're nowhere near $2.5 million. To sell $1 million worth of real estate then meant selling the equivalent of more than seven average-priced houses a month.

And that's what I did. With that goal in front of me daily, I soon quadrupled my sales. The days of cutting corners and staving off creditors were gone. If I took Linda back to the pizzeria at Van Dyke and Lynch, it was because we liked the food, and not because we couldn't afford better.

A CALL TO GREATNESS

Floyd Wickman became a successful speaker the same way he became a successful real estate salesperson. First came the awareness, and he remembers very well the moment he glimpsed that possibility.

It was April 16, 1974. Floyd had hit the top as a real estate salesman and had been into sales management.

On that day, he went to a seminar in downtown Detroit as one of 2,300 participants. The speaker was J. Douglas Edwards, the grandfather of sales techniques. Any salesman worth his salt at that time knew Doug Edwards.

As Edwards looked out over that large audience, he made a statement that sent Floyd spinning off in a new direction.

"One of you has greatness in you," he said.

"I swear to God, I think he's talking to me," thought Floyd. It was as if an inner voice were telling the young Wickman, 'You want to do what he's doing."

AN AUDIENCE OF 2,300 BY APRIL 1979

Now remember that at this point Floyd was just the branch manager for a dinky little real estate company in Farmington, Michigan. He had never spoken to a crowd—never done any public speaking.

But he was somehow inspired by the spectacle of this man standing before a crowd of 2,300 people and imparting knowledge and inspiration. He looked at Doug Edwards. He was about Floyd's size—just under 6 feet, weighing between 170 and 180 pounds. Floyd could see himself standing up there just as Edwards was.

That night, Floyd wrote down on a piece of paper:

> *"I will speak in front of 2,300 people by April 16, 1979.*
> *"(Signed) Floyd Wickman."*

Floyd started showing it to everybody. It seemed like an impossible dream. He is not an extrovert who enjoys mixing and mingling. He likes people, but interacting with a crowd drains him of energy. Yet, things started happening that moved him toward his goal. He got out of real estate sales management and into training. He eventually became training director for a nationwide real estate company. In February of 1979, the company held its annual sales convention in Las Vegas. There were 2,600 people present to hear the keynote speaker. The keynote speaker was a guy named Floyd Wickman. He had beat his deadline by two months.

ZIG ZIGLAR'S FORMULA

Zig Ziglar, that master of motivation, had helped steer Floyd toward that goal.

Bob Mohr of Master Marketing Association, who had brought J. Douglas Edwards to Detroit, came to Floyd to sell some tickets to a program featuring Ziglar.

By then, Floyd was director of training for Lee Real Estate, and was the guy to see if you wanted to get the Lee people to turn out for a program.

"I'll make you a deal Bob," Floyd said. "If a hundred percent of our people buy a ticket, will you arrange dinner with Zig Ziglar and me?"

"It's a deal," said Mohr.

Floyd didn't quite deliver the 100%, but it was a solid 90%—the highest participation ever from his company. Bob didn't get him a dinner with Zig, but he did manage a breakfast. To Floyd, it was like having breakfast with God.

"I have a goal," he told Zig. "By April 1979, I want to address an audience of 2,300 people. If you could give me one piece of advice, what would it be?"

Floyd had been collecting advice from every possible source, and he had done an article for a professional journal on about a dozen pieces of wisdom.

None of them quite had the impact of Ziglar's wisdom.

"Sure Floyd, I'll give you some advice," he said.

He reached into his briefcase and pulled out a copy of his book, See You at the Top.

He opened it and signed something in the front. When he handed it back, Floyd looked at what he had written. It read:

"You're a winner. John 15:5–7."

"There's your advice," he said.

Floyd stared at it in puzzlement. He had been reared in the Catholic Church, but that didn't mean he had paid close attention to the priest's homilies, and he surely didn't spend a lot of time reading the Bible on his own.

As far as he was concerned, John 15:5–7 might have been an incomplete telephone number.

Floyd went home feeling about like the Pharaoh must have

felt before Joseph explained the meaning of his dreams about the lean years and the fat years.

"Linda," he said, "Do we have a Bible in the house?"

"Not that I know of," she said. She must have thought Floyd had really done something to repent for this time.

Where had he last seen a Bible?

His mother had one. Of course!

Floyd called her.

"Mom, can I borrow your Bible?"

She must have thought all her prayers had been answered. At last, Floyd was coming home to the church.

Floyd took the Bible home.

"Do you know where John is?" he asked Linda.

"It's in the New Testament with the other Gospels, Matthew, Mark and Luke."

Floyd fumbled until he came to John's Gospel, then turned to the 15th chapter and the fifth through the seventh verses.

Floyd wasn't sure exactly what to expect. Was it some magic formula? Or maybe some explicit directions such as "Go ye to the Detroit Chamber of Commerce Convention Bureau and inquire ye whereof the largest organizations have need for speakers, and lo, thou shalt receive an invitation"?

Within the scriptural citation he found a powerful piece of advice that was even briefer than Zig's note in the front of the book. It read:

Ask and Ye Shall Receive.

What Floyd began to realize was that the way to "ask" is to set a goal and commit yourself to fulfilling it. When you do that, things start to happen.

In Floyd's case, things started to happen immediately.

He became so fascinated with his mother's Bible that he couldn't put it down. He read John 15:5–7, and then kept reading—until 3 o'clock in the morning. It was the first time he had ever read the Bible.

Floyd wasn't a religious man by any stretch of the imagination. But here's what happened:

The next morning at 9 o'clock he was sitting in his office. The phone rang. It was Dennis Galloway. He and Henry Schmidt had just bought the region for the Realty World franchise.

"I understand you're a pretty good trainer," Denny said. "Would you be interested in being a regional trainer?"

This was an opportunity to go to work for what was to become an 80-office franchise. At the time Floyd was working with only seven offices.

He became a regional training director for Realty World, which meant he was making more money. More importantly, he started expanding. His name became known to more people. After a little more than two years, he became Realty World's national training director. All of a sudden, he was connected to hundreds of offices throughout the United States and Canada.

Realty World didn't realize it, but it had created a monster by letting him travel and practice his speeches while in their employ. After Floyd went on to other things, the company stopped letting the national training director go out and do speeches.

Floyd made those speeches because he was practicing for that big moment when he would step out on that platform to talk to 2,300 people. Make that 2,600.

MAKE THOSE GOALS SPECIFIC

Have you noticed anything about the goals we've been talking about?

For openers, the goals were **specific.** I didn't come away from that STI training course and pledge, "I'm going to improve my sales performance."

I came back and said, "I'm going to make the Million-Dollar Club."

When Doug Edwards issued his call to greatness, I didn't decide, "I'm going to be a successful speaker too."

I said, "I'm going to address an audience of 2,300 people by April 16, 1979."

To repeat: The goals were specific. They have to be specific or you'll never hit them.

DON'T JUST AIM FOR 'SOMEWHERE'

I'm going to risk becoming redundant, but it's my way of reinforcing for you the importance of some of the points I'm making about goals. So here comes another illustration about goals.

Suppose the people at NASA had told the Apollo astronauts, "We're going to point this sucker toward the sky, fellows. Go out and land on some other world. We're behind you guys. Bye."

With that kind of target, the Eagle would never have landed. The Apollo space craft was aimed toward the moon and, in fact, toward a specific spot on the moon. Had NASA simply aimed it toward the sky, it would still be drifting in space.

So when you're setting goals, zero in on a bullseye. Don't just say, "I'm going to increase my sales next month." Say, "I'm going to call on 100 people in the next month. Out of that 100, I will enter into a deal with 20. Out of that 20, I'll close on two."

Specific goals not only give you a target to shoot for. They also give you something to visualize. A visible goal is always easier to achieve.

Have you ever done any mountain climbing? If you have, you know how hard it is to put one foot ahead of the other when the climb is steep and you can see nothing ahead but rocks and trees.

But when you finally reach a clearing and look up and see the peak—your goal—your energy is recharged. You can see what you're struggling toward. You can see it getting closer. You know what it's going to take to get there, and you know you've got what it takes.

You know, too, that an offensive football team is harder to stop inside the opponent's 15-yard line than it is on its own 20. Why? Because the goal is in sight. There's an extra incentive to move the ball.

MAKE THEM ATTAINABLE

Goals should be ambitious but **attainable.** When you decide to become successful as a real estate salesperson, you don't say, "Next week I'm going to sell the world's tallest building." You say, "Next year I'm going to make the Million Dollar Club." Making the Million Dollar Club in the late '60s meant selling around 88 houses. You can't sell 88 houses in a day or in a week. But if you hustle and work smart, you can sell one, two or three houses a week for 52 weeks, and that could get you into the Million Dollar Club for the year.

When I decided to become a speaker, I didn't make it my goal to address a crowd of 2,300 next week, next month or next year. I gave myself five years. The goal was no snap, but it was attainable.

Take stock of where you are and what you have. Then set a specific, **attainable** goal.

MAKE THEM YOUR GOALS

The goals you set should be **your** goals. Had H.B. told me to sell a million dollars' worth of real estate or hit the road, I might have looked for some other line of work. His ultimatum might have motivated me to work harder, but I would have hated it.

Had Linda pestered me to become a public speaker, I might have laughed it off.

But both those goals represented things **I** wanted to do.

In my woodworking hobby, people often ask me to make things for them. I try to accommodate, but sometimes I just can't get started. Even when Linda wants me to make her something, it takes me forever, and I don't even enjoy it that much.

But let me get started on something **I** decide to make, and you can't pull me away from it. Linda calls out, "Honey, come on up. It's one o'clock in the morning," and I say, "I'll just be another hour."

If you're working on somebody else's project, working until 1 A.M. is burning the candle at both ends. But when it's your goal, it's as if your energy were coming from a breeder reactor that creates fuel faster than it consumes it.

When you're working toward your own goals, you never feel pressured. You are propelled by positive stress—the kind that motivates you to do your best without filling you with anxiety over the possibility of failure.

Negative stress comes from trying to meet goals somebody else has set for you.

My company has dozens of trainers in its teaching program. If you're a trainer, I'm not going to tell you how many students to take. I'll say, "You tell me how many students you want to do next year. How many are you comfortable with?"

When you give me a number, I'm not going to try to raise it. All I ask is that you do what you tell me you'll do. I won't put the pressure on you. We've made that mistake in the past; that's why it's so clear in my mind.

PUT IT IN WRITING

Finally, **put the goal in writing.** This is important. If you just set a **mental** goal, you're writing it in air. It disappears as soon as your mind turns to other subjects. Saying it aloud is a little better. The spoken word is soon forgotten.

Writing it down preserves and reinforces. It enables you to be more specific. When you put something on paper, you can sharpen it and refine until it's just the way you want it. You won't be asking yourself, "Did I say April 16, 1975 or April 16, 1979? Did I say 2,300 people or 1,300?" You've got it in writing. You can look at it again and again.

Also, putting it in writing is the first step in the commitment process. Commitments are put in writing, whether you're talking about international treaties, real estate contracts or the form you sign when you're charging your lunch on your Visa card. When you show this written commitment to friends, you're putting your credibility on the line.

Start with a 3X5-inch card. Write your goal on it. You won't have much room, so keep it simple and clear. Put that card where it's always in sight.

Next, take out a sheet of paper and write your goal across the top. Then write down the things you're going to do to achieve that goal. Whenever you feel like playing golf or going to the beach or taking the day off instead of prospecting, take out that sheet of paper. This paper will remind you where your chosen priorities lie.

MAKE IT SOMETHING YOU WANT

What goals should you set?

To answer that question, you have to ask another: What do you want?

That was the question Floyd had to help Phyllis answer.

Phyllis was a real estate salesperson in one of Floyd's training programs. She was having incredible difficulty setting her goals.

"What is it you really want?" Floyd asked her.

"I don't know, Floyd. I've got everything I could ask for."

"Wouldn't you like a little extra money to spend?"

"Not really. I don't actually need this job; my husband earns enough to support both of us."

"How about a nicer home?"

"We love the home we have."

"What do you do in your spare time, Phyllis?"

"Oh, nothing spectacular. We're a typical middle-class suburban couple. We enjoy eating out, a little travel, and doing things with the people at our church."

"So you're active in the church."

"Yes, we really are. In fact, my husband is on the building committee."

"What are you building."

"We're ready to build a new sanctuary. It's really going to be an impressive structure; you should see the architect's drawings. But it's going to be 'touch and go' coming up with the money. I was just saying to Claude the other day that we ought to give some ourselves."

"How much would you like to give?"

Her eyes lit up.

"I'd like to give $10,000."

"Sounds to me like you've got a goal," Floyd said.

He encouraged her to write it down: "I am going to give $10,000 to the building fund of my church."

She did better than that. She drew a picture of the church. She put herself in the picture—handing the minister a check for $10,000.

She and Floyd worked out a step-by-step plan for attaining her goal.

Did Phyllis make the $10,000 for her church?

Oh ye of little faith! Verily, verily I say unto thee: You bet your life she did.

How did she do it? She set a goal. It was **her** goal—not mine, not her husband's, not her preacher's. It was a specific goal: $10,000 is pretty specific. It was attainable. Sure, $10,000 is a lot of bread for most real estate salespeople, but it's not Fort Knox. She wrote down her goal, and even drew a picture, better to visualize what she wanted to accomplish. She wrote down the steps she planned to take to achieve it.

And of course she went out and worked for the money.

IT'S TIME YOU MET DOMINICO

At this point, it's time you met Dominico Siciliano.

Dominico is a hard fellow to work into a book on how to sell real estate. That's because he breaks all of the rules, fits none of the molds and drives people like me up the wall.

> *Dominico answered a recruiting ad Floyd had run for an office in Pleasant Ridge, Michigan. Floyd knew within 10 seconds that he didn't want to hire him.*
>
> *For one thing, he looked as if he had just got off a tramp steamer from Sicily, having slept in his suit the whole distance.*
>
> *For another thing, he was overbearing.*
>
> *The clincher was that he couldn't speak English—at least not in any dialect Floyd could understand.*
>
> *"You geeva me da chance, I sella your houses," Dominico promised.*
>
> *"Gee, Mr. Siciliano, we admire your initiative and we'd like to hire you, but we're looking for someone more experienced in the real estate business," said Floyd.*
>
> *"I know all about da real estate," he said. "I'ma borna in a house, I'ma raised in a house; I know all abouta da houses. You geeva me da job, I sella your houses."*

It was hard to argue with Dominico about that. It was hard to argue with Dominico about anything. How can you argue with a guy when you can understand only every third word?

Floyd turned him away that first day, but he came back. Again and again.

At last, Floyd handed him an application, knowing that before he could come to work he would have to pass the real estate examination, and that real estate examinations, in Michigan, are given in English.

"Dominico," Floyd said, "You go to school and study hard. And if you pass the test, give me a call."

Several months passed, and the memory of Dominico faded. Then came the telephone call.

"Allo, Meester Floyd. Thees ees Dominico. I no pass-a da test."

"Gee, that's too bad, Dominico," Floyd said, trying to hide his relief.

"Dat's-a right," he agreed. "It's-a too bad-a. But for you, Meester Floyd, I keep-a trying."

Dominico took the test two more times, and flunked both times. In Michigan, it's three strikes and you're out on the real estate exam, unless you're handicapped, which Dominico wasn't, or you get special permission from the state board, which Dominico did.

On his fourth try, Dominico made the same score Floyd had made on his first exam: 75. That's the lowest score you can make and pass, but it's also the highest score you have to make to sell real estate.

Dominico called Floyd once more, gave him the good news, and reminded him of his promise. Floyd Wickman doesn't lie, although sometimes he is sorely tempted. He hired Dominico.

That first year Dominico closed 94 transactions. Floyd has seen office staffs with a dozen or more agents who didn't generate that much business.

How did he do it?

"I finda somebody who wants-a to sell-a da house. I finda somebody who wants-a to buy-a da house. I say, 'You wanna sell? Okay. You wanna buy? Okay.' "

A NEW SUIT EVERY MONTH

Now what was I talking about before Dominico came along?

Oh yes. Goals. Dominico had goals.

His goal was not to sell 94 houses a year or to make the Million-Dollar Club. Nothing that grand.

At that time, the top salesman each month won a new suit. Dominico made it his goal to win the suit each month.

He had the best wardrobe in the office. When he wore the suits, they still looked as if he had slept in them all the way from the Mediterranean to the Great Lakes, but they were great suits. And Dominico was a great salesman and, I might add, one of the nicest men I've ever met.

Dominico's goal was simple and attainable. All he had to do was outsell every salesman in the office for one month. I had already learned how hard it was to say no to Dominico. It seemed that buyers and sellers of real estate had just as much trouble.

If your goal is a new suit every month, let it pull you toward success. If your goal is a Salesperson of the Month plaque, let that pull you toward success.

Plaques are great instruments for encouraging goal-setting in the sales business. They always represent clear-cut, specific, attainable goals. They're the proof that you made it. They don't buy groceries and they don't pay the rent. But what you do to get them will keep you eating and will keep a roof over your head. Maybe people should create those plaques in their own minds. Or maybe they should go out and buy some plaques.

The woman who wants to lose weight, for instance, might buy a plaque that reads, "Skinniest Woman on Earth." She might give it to her husband or boyfriend and have him present it to her when she's attained her goal.

But most people set loftier goals than bronze plaques. Sometimes the goals are too lofty to be practical. If you find that you've bitten off more than you can chew, don't get discouraged. If your goal was $1 million in sales and $989,000 was the best you could do, relax; you won't go to hell for that.

WHEN THE GOAL SEEMS TOO HIGH

Let's say that your goal is to buy a new automobile during the next year and pay cash for it. When you think of a new car, you're not thinking of the Lullaby Four that your Aunt Patricia drives to meetings of her sewing circle. You're thinking of that six-liter job with the vibrators in the front seat, wet bar in the back, and a compact disc player hooked to a 16-speaker stereo system that makes you think you're surrounded by the Boston Pops. The kind of chariot that will set you back 35 G's at least.

But you have only $17,000 in hand, including the cash Uncle Harry left you when he passed to his reward, the money you've been saving for the trip to Hawaii, the cash value of your life-insurance policy, and the value of your present car.

No two ways about it. If your goal is to buy that gorgeous set of wheels during the next 12 months, you're going to have to come up with $18,000 above your normal living expenses.

But that's your goal; you wrote it down last night. This morning you've got to figure out how to reach it.

The math isn't really that complicated. To earn an extra $18,000 a year means that you've got to earn an extra $4,500 a quarter, which comes to $1,500 a month, or about $348.85 per week.

Can you earn that extra $348.85 per week on average for the next 52 weeks?

Let's say it's going to take two sales per week to generate that extra $348.85. You figure you can get them by developing 10 additional prospects from the 50 additional people you'll talk to each week. Can you work in those 50 additional contacts? You know your own capacities and you know the demands on your time and wallet. Maybe it's not realistic.

Should you trash your goal then?

Of course not. Maybe you can wait another six months for the new car. That means you can buy it by earning an extra $1,000 a month or $232.55 a week.

Don't make a habit of setting extravagant goals, then backing off. But if you decide on a goal and find, in the cold light of day, that it's an impossible dream, there's just one thing to do: Get real. Adjust your goal to fit the possibilities. But don't sell yourself short.

FOLLOW THE VISION

Let's say you've decided to go for the bomb. That 35-grand baby is down in the showroom with your name on it. You know what you're going to have to do to get it, and you've determined that it's doable.

How can you keep your mind focused on the goal?

Get a picture of that car. The dealer will have full-color brochures, illustrating your choice of colors, interiors and options.

Put that picture where you can see it every day. Visualize it as you do your prospecting and make your presentations. The vision will lead you toward the goal.

THE GATEWAY IN YOUR BRAIN

Goals are nothing more than the codification of your dreams. They take dreams out of the realm of fantasy and put them into the realm of reality.

To understand how this happens, you have to know a little bit about how the brain works. So listen to Floyd the shrink, the guy who got his Ph.D. in psychology on the east side of Detroit, where Ph.D. stood for "Plenty Hip Dude."

Dreams are born in the right side of the brain. Goals are set in the left side of your brain. To translate your dreams into reality, you have to open the gate between your left brain and your right brain.

Dreams come out of your intuition. Goals come out of your logic. Stick with me a little longer while I explain the difference.

DIFFERENT KINDS OF SMARTS

You don't have to hold a Ph.D. to know that there are several kinds of smarts. One kind is scholastic smarts. Certain people are gifted with this kind of smarts. They're the ones who do great in school, because they like to read and they understand what they read. Their minds follow clear, logical paths. The fancy term for that is linear reasoning: If you give them a cause, they can figure out the effect, and vice versa. They make good mathematicians, good lawyers, good planners.

Such a person tends to use the left side of the brain more than the right side. The left side of the brain is the logical, reasoning side. The right brain is the creative, intuitive side.

When left-brain people seek to solve problems, they're like oil prospectors, who assemble all the geological data and aerial surveys and carefully plot the location of the oil. Then they drill where the facts tell them they'll find the oil. Left-brain thinkers take out pencils and pads, or calculators and computers, and they shut themselves up in their rooms. They organize their facts, and through logical reasoning they slowly but surely zero in on the truth.

When right-brain people seek to solve problems, it's like panning for gold. They slowly swirl things around in their minds, running the waters of insight over the muddy facts until something glitters. They don't find that shiny nugget of truth through careful calculation and deduction. The find it through intuition. They don't need to be in an office or laboratory. They can do their mental panning while going for quiet walks, or while reclining beside a stream.

THINKERS AND DREAMERS

Laws and regulations are drafted by left-brain thinkers. Poems and symphonies are composed by right-brain dreamers. Can you imagine a symphony composed according to scientific logic? Can you imagine a building code drafted by poetic dreamers? The inspiration for a building code may originate in the right brain. But it takes the left brain to organize the details; to dot the i's and cross the t's. A symphony has to follow certain rules dictated by the laws of the musical scale. But for it to accomplish its purpose, which is to stir human emotions, it has to come from the creative corners of the right brain.

When people first started measuring intelligence, they measured the logical intelligence housed in the left side of the brain.

But as time passed, smart people began to realize that there were other types of intelligence, and that these too could propel a person to success.

Harvard Psychologist Howard Gardner divides human intelligence into seven categories. Only one of them—the logical-mathematical type of intelligence, is found in the left brain.

RIGHT-BRAIN INTELLIGENCES

The six others are right-brain intelligences. Creative writing comes from the right side of the brain. So does the ability to visualize objects and manipulate them in the mind—the intelligence needed by sculptors, architects and designers of machinery. The ability to make body and mind work together in dancing and athletics is a right-brain intelligence. So is the ability to "read" other people intuitively. The ability to know and understand oneself is also a right-brain gift, as is the musician's sensitivity to pitch, melody, rhythm and tone.

Now, all six of these right-brain intelligences are extremely important. But intelligence for most of our modern age has been equated with learning. Learning, for most of the present millennium, has come from reading books. And reading books is a left-brain skill.

Therefore, people who do most of their thinking in the right side of the brain have tended to be underestimated. Thomas Edison, Winston Churchill and Albert Einstein were right-brain people who were thought to be rather dull intellectually until they presented unarguable evidence to the contrary.

Logical people tend to accept the world the way it is and try to adapt to it. Creative people are never satisfied with the way things are. They try to adapt the world to fit their desires. The logical mind is more interested in what exists. The creative mind is more interested in what is possible.

George Bernard Shaw had one of his characters speak the words that could very well be the right brain speaking to the left:

"You see things; and you say, 'Why?' But I dream things that never were; and I say, 'Why not?' "

TRUTH THROUGH INTUITION

One reason that right-brain people are often underestimated is that they seem so illogical. But experience has shown that the logical mind is not the only route to truth and learning. The right brain transcends logic to find the truth through intuition.

Logical people are prone to scoff at dreamers because their dreams conflict with the logical view of the universe.

"Did you hear what that idiot Copernicus said? He claims the sun doesn't move around the earth, but the earth moves around the sun. Any fool can see that it's the sun that moves."

"Look at that oddball Columbus, sailing westward to find the East. Common sense tells you that if the earth were shaped like a ball, we'd all fall off."

"That nut Thomas Jefferson thinks the common people are capable of governing themselves. How can you get intelligent laws out of ignorant people of average intellect?"

"Have you seen those kooky Wright brothers? They think they can put a motor on a pair of wings and make their contraption fly."

Any logical person who looks at the heavy body and flimsy wings of a bumblebee knows that the varmint can't fly.

But the bumblebee dreams of flowers and nectar, sets its wings in motion—and flies.

So to sum it up: It takes the creative right brain to dream up ideas that were never thought of before.

But it takes the logical left brain to devise practical steps to turn the ideas into reality.

OPENING THE GATE

The truth is, we all function in both sides of our brains. Most of us prefer one side over the other, but we all can learn to use both sides of the brain. Right-brain thinkers who are good at dreaming up ideas but lax about implementing them can cultivate the left-brain skills they need to turn ideas into reality.

And left-brain people can become more creative by opening

the gateways to their right brains. Creativity is nothing more than the ability to trust your imagination.

So what opens that gate between the left and right sides of your brain?

The same thing that opens a literal gate: somebody or something that is pushing to get through.

When you become aware of possibilities, let your right brain dream its dreams. Trust your dreams. That trust will allow the dreams to enter your left brain, where your logical intelligence can go to work on a plan for converting your dream to reality.

Now the dreams in your right brain are feeding the reasoning powers of your left brain. The two sides of your brain are communicating.

Remember, too, that the right side of your brain is the one that's in touch with your subconscious. Keep focusing on positive dreams, and your subconscious will create for you the habits and attitudes that lead to success.

Try this:

Find yourself the quietest, most comfortable spot in the house. Sit back, relax and turn off the lights. Now start picturing the things you want to have, the person you want to be and the places you want to go.

Forget the room, the chair, the airplane overhead, the bills on your desk, your appointments for tomorrow. Just relax and let your senses take over.

If you want a condominium on the seashore, hear the waves and the seagulls; smell the salt air and feel the warmth of the sun. If you make these things live in your dreams, you have taken the first step toward making your dream a reality.

Let's say you're a salesperson and your performance has been mediocre. That same quiet spot and comfortable chair can be your transport to success. Sit back and experience in your mind what it would be like to be the top sales producer in your company or your division. How would you like to receive a plaque for top sales production in front of 500 of your peers? Visualize the ballroom and the head table. See yourself shaking hands with the president of the company as you're handed your plaque. Hear the sound of 1,000 hands clapping together as they applaud **YOU.**

If you can dream it, you can accomplish it.

So if you've been wallowing in mediocrity, take a look around you and become aware of the opportunities for greatness. Then set yourself a goal of greatness. Make it a specific goal. Make it ambitious, but attainable. Make it **your** goal and not a goal somebody else wants you to attain. Write it down, and keep it before you as you go about your work. Visualize the fulfillment of your goal. Dream of greatness, and believe your dreams. When you do this, you will be activating the intuitive smarts in your right brain. This will open the gateway between your right brain and your left brain, which houses your logical smarts. Your logical left brain then will go to work to bring to reality the dreams it receives from your right brain.

You will then be ready to take the third of the **Seven Steps to Achieving Your Full Potential.**

List the most important points you have gained from the preceding Step:

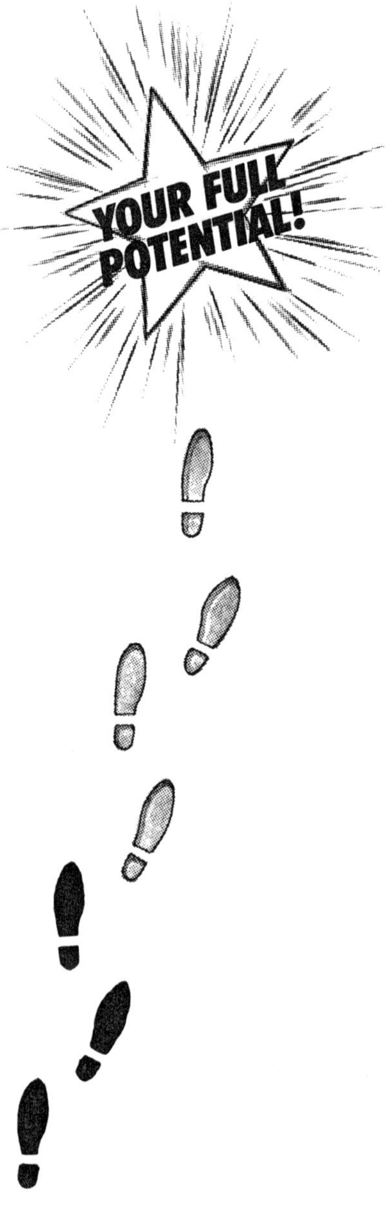
YOUR FULL POTENTIAL!

Step Three

Make a Commitment

The third step toward greatness is commitment.

Commitment is the logical follow-up to awareness and goal-setting.

Awareness is "can do."

Goal-setting is "want to."

Commitment is "have to."

Look it up in Webster's. To commit oneself, it says, is to "speak or act in such a manner as to bind oneself to a certain line of conduct." Notice the word "bind." It doesn't say anything like "subject to the following conditions." That's not commitment; that's equivocation. As Casey Stengel would say, "You could look it up."

Commitment is what those American soldiers had when the Germans surrounded them at the Belgian town of Bastogne.

The Nazi general offered them an alternative: Surrender and they wouldn't be wiped out.

The answer came in a one-word message: "Nuts."

That was commitment. And the Wehrmacht soon learned what an encircled American army can do when it's committed.

The Russians were in an even more desperate situation at the battle of Stalingrad. The Volga River was the last barrier holding back the Nazi tanks that were aimed at the Soviet heart. If the Red Army retreated across the Volga, the Hun would cross, and the rape of Mother Russia would be all but accomplished.

The word that went down to the Russian soldiers was this: "There is no other side of the river."

That was commitment. Not to the preservation of communism; not to the glory of Marshal Stalin, but to the salvation of Mother Russia. And the German army suffered one of its most disastrous defeats of World War II.

Iraqi President Saddam Hussein also learned about commitment the hard way. He was told to get out of Kuwait. But he was committed to holding on to the little oil-rich country. President George Bush, the American people and our coalition partners were committed to getting him out. Saddam Hussein didn't believe the commitment was there. He was convinced that his elite Republican Guard could make a coalition victory so costly that the Americans and their international partners would not challenge him.

But Bush backed his commitment with action. He refused to let Saddam Hussein deter him with threats of poison gas or nuclear weapons. He put an Army, a Navy, an Air Force and Marines into the Middle East. Those forces consisted of men and women committed to their mission. They did their jobs like accomplished pros. They demonstrated courage born of commitment. As the relentless air war began its systematic demolition of the Iraqi military forces, Saddam tried to goad the coalition into a premature ground attack. But the coalition remained committed to its master plan.

In the end, it was the Iraqis who demonstrated a lack of commitment. Having no cause they believed in very deeply, Saddam's military leaders deserted their troops in private automobiles. And the rank-and-file Iraqi soldiers surrendered in droves.

Until you make that commitment, your dreams are nothing but fantasy. Once you've made it, they're on their way to reality.

When you've made a commitment, you've put your whole being on the line, which brings me to the story of the chicken and the pig who were thinking of opening a restaurant.

"We'll cater to the breakfast crowd," said the chicken. "We'll serve the best ham and eggs in town. Are we partners?"

"I'll have to think about it," said the pig. "After all, it would only call for a contribution from you. From me, it would require a total commitment."

Think about that the next time you're enjoying ham and eggs. But remember: You don't have to serve yourself up on a platter. Your can commit yourself to serve in much more rewarding ways.

BURN YOUR BRIDGES

One sure way to commit yourself is to burn your bridges. That's what I was doing that evening when I took Linda to the pizzeria and told her I was going to the top. That was a commitment. It wasn't just a commitment to Linda; I was making one to myself as well. I was burning my bridges. I was leaving myself no avenue for retreat.

That can be a little scary. But if you don't burn your bridges, you'll never move on toward new goals. You'll be like Tony, who ran Tony's Market two doors down from us when I was a kid.

Tony and his wife, Rosa, were always arguing.

Tony would walk around the store muttering in his Italian accent, "Some day I'm gonna leave that woman."

That's what he would be saying when he cut you a wedge of cheese: "Some day I'm gonna leave that woman."

That's what he would be saying as he handed you your change: "Some day I'm gonna leave that woman."

One day it appeared that Tony was putting some commitment behind his statement. It must have been 2:30 A.M., and you could hear the shouts and the threats, and finally a door slamming.

A couple of seconds later you could hear Rosa's voice.

"Hey, Tony, what am I gonna do with your suits?"

"Ah, give 'em to your brother."

"Hey Tony, what am I gonna do with your car?"

"Ah, give it to your brother."

And then:

"Hey Tony, what am I gonna do all alone on those cold winter nights?"

The pause was longer than usual. Then you could hear Tony shuffling back, saying, "Some day I'm gonna leave that woman."

'IF I COME BACK, SHOOT ME'

Suppose you've decided to leave your job and go on to another opportunity.

So you walk in to the boss and say:

"Hey boss, It's been nice, but a new opportunity has been offered me. I'd like to give it a try, but I'd appreciate it if you'd leave the door open for me just in case it doesn't work out."

If you leave on that note, you know it won't work out. The first little failure on the new job—and there are always little failures—will send you packing for home.

Commitment is when you go to your boss and say, "Boss, I've been offered a new job and I'm taking it. I know it involves some risks, but I'm gonna make a go of it. So don't hold my seat for me. If I ever walk in the door again and ask for my job back, shoot me on the spot. As a matter of fact, here, I'm leaving this gun with you. There's a bullet in the chamber. Use it if you see me coming back asking for my job."

Unless you're willing to make that kind of commitment, you're like a person who tries to win a tug of war by pulling on both ends of the rope. You may be putting forth some effort, but you're not going anywhere either way.

MAKE IT PUBLIC

You aren't committed when you shove back in your recliner and say to yourself, "I'm going to do it."

You're committed when you broadcast the news: "Hey world, I'm gonna do this thing."

Commitment is what Babe Ruth had on October 1, 1932, in the fifth inning of the World Series between the New York Yankees and the Chicago Cubs.

The game was tied 4–4 when the Babe came to bat. The Bambino had already made up his mind that he was going to hit a home run.

The Babe was aware of the possibility. After all, he had hit 60 home runs in one season five years earlier and had been ripping along in the 40s and 50s every season since.

So this time up, he set a goal of hitting a home run and breaking the tie. Did he keep that goal to himself?

No. Babe made a commitment. When Cubs pitcher Charlie Root whipped the first two pitches past him, Babe called them as strikes, even before the umpire did. He watched as Root wasted two pitches.

Then he announced his commitment. He pointed toward the flagpole in centerfield, so that all the fans could see him. Everybody in that ballpark understood what the Babe was saying: He intended to put the next pitch into the centerfield stands. That was commitment.

Had Babe struck out—as he often did—he would have had a lot of egg on his face. He had painted himself into a corner. It was either put up or shut up. A single wouldn't do it. A double against the right-field wall wouldn't do it. It was a home run or a large helping of crow.

So Babe hit the home run—just a few feet to one side of the flagpole.

Making that commitment did several things for Ruth.

For one thing, it forced him to focus on the goal he had set. He couldn't think about yesterday's game. He couldn't think about who would be pitching tomorrow. He couldn't think about the tied score. He had to think about bringing the fat part of his bat solidly into contact with the ball, launching it into the center-field stands.

For another thing, it rallied Babe's fans to his support. Their cheers would help bring him to just the right state of arousal to accomplish the athletic feat he had set out to accomplish.

For still another thing, it put the Cubs fans on notice: He was going to make believers of them. Sure they would razz him and cheer for Root to strike him out. Do you think the Babe cared? It gave him all the more reason to clobber the ball.

USE YOUR ACQUAINTANCES ON THE SIDELINES

Let me pass on another little tidbit from Floyd Wickman, Ph.D. (Remember, the name's Floyd, not Freud, and in this case the Ph.D stands for Piping Hot Deals): One out of every four persons who know you hopes you will fall flat on your face. One out of four would like to see you succeed. The rest—that's half of your acquaintances—don't care whether you hit a home run or strike out.

That can be a useful piece of information for you. Most people worry about the 50% who couldn't care less. They're afraid that if those fence-straddlers ever make up their minds, they'll come down on the wrong side. So most people adjust their behavior so that half their acquaintances will remain in neutral corners.

BLENDING WITH THE CATS

That's what Floyd was doing for the first 26 years of his life. His friends were cats, so he acted like a cat so that he wouldn't stand out from the crowd. If you stand out from the crowd, people have to make up their minds whether they like you or not. And Floyd didn't want the undecideds to make up their minds to dislike him.

Once he became aware, set his goals, and made his commitment, he cut loose from the pack. He didn't care whether those fence-straddlers liked him or not. His attention was now focused on the other two groups.

How could they help him?

By putting some positive stress into his life.

LET POSITIVE STRESS CHALLENGE YOU

Everybody thinks of stress as **THE ENEMY**—that ugly something that makes you break into rashes; that causes you to have nervous breakdowns; that gives you strokes and heart attacks and cancer.

That's the dark side of The Force. There's a bright side too.

The human system needs stress in the form of challenge. The unchallenged person will simply wither away. The brain finds no further reason to keep the body alive. Watch people after they retire. The person who retreats to a rocking chair and lives on a comfortable pension had better enjoy the peace and tranquility while it's possible, because such a person probably will live only three years or so after retirement. It's the active retirees constantly seeking challenge—whether through hobbies, new careers or helping others—who live into their 80s and 90s.

What does this have to do with you, the young-to-middle-aged person still looking for success?

It means that you need to find a source of positive stress.

Your friends—that 25% of your acquaintances who wish you well—can provide that challenge. When an athletic team is playing in its home park, the cheers of the crowd provide an extra boost that can make the difference between victory and defeat. That's positive stress.

When soldiers in combat get packages and cards from home; when Bob Hope takes the trouble to bring pretty girls, songs and gags into the battle zone for them, their morale soars. They get a good jolt of positive stress. Here's something worth fighting for.

Why do you think I took Linda to the pizzeria and told her of my commitment? Just because I like Italian food? I wanted to benefit from the positive stress she could put in my life just by believing me and encouraging me.

But if you're just relying on your friends, you're getting a boost from only one out of four of your acquaintances. Where do you go for additional challenge?

LET THE NAY-SAYERS HELP YOU

Try looking into that other crowd—the 25% who are hoping you'll fall on your face.

How can they give you positive stress?

By giving you an incentive to prove them wrong, to make them eat crow, to show them what you're made of. Why do you think Mr. Holt, my old principal at Osborne High School, has been such an inspiration to me?

Because he told my mother I was a loser. Every time I get into my Mercedes or my limousine, I want to say "Thank you, Mr. Holt."

When the critics start their cackling, let that be an incentive to make you work harder. Do you think it bothered Wilbur and Orville Wright when the critics jeered, "It'll never fly"?

Nobody ever built a monument to a critic. Next time you're flying down the eastern seaboard, take a close look down in the vicinity of Kitty Hawk, North Carolina. You'll see an impressive monument to the Wright Brothers.

One of the most stressful activities anybody ever took up was the French Underground of World War II. Its members lived in sewers, ate terrible food and flirted with death every moment of their lives. They knew that if they were caught they would be shot on the spot.

Their Nazi enemies gave them the challenge they needed to surmount the hardships, maintain good health, and eventually share in the Allied victory.

So use your enemies as a source of positive stress. You can do it by making a commitment and letting everybody know about it.

What do you think happened when I advertised the fact that I was going to follow up my dismal first year on the job with a million dollar sales performance?

My wife and friends said, "Atta boy Floyd. We'll help you in every way we can."

And they did. They reminded me to make more sales calls. They reminded me to keep my customers happy. They helped me with tips on presentations and prospecting and qualifying and closing.

My sorehead acquaintances said, "Million Dollar Club eh? How much did you earn last year? $4,200? Well, I've heard that pigs can fly, but the only one I saw that tried it landed face first in the mud."

You know how that goes.

Of course, there were all those other people who figured that whatever I did was no skin off their backs.

The good news is that although those people didn't help me physically, they did help me. They gave me an incentive to make them stand up and take notice.

INTO SALES MANAGEMENT

So with a little boost from his friends and a little goad from his critics, Floyd hit the top in real estate sales. He made the Million Dollar Club repeatedly. He didn't know it then, but his production put him in the top 0.1% in the industry.

If there had been a Two Million Dollar Club, Floyd would have made it too. He approached that figure on several occasions, but since $1 million was the figure that got the recognition, Floyd decided it was time to move on to other challenges.

In four years, he rose from a down-and-out, non-productive hack of a salesperson to become sales manager for his office at Lee Real Estate.

And he was a good sales manager. He had gone from being "the undertaker" to being a Pete Rose. That means he was a playing manager. He sold real estate and he managed real estate salespeople. In eight and a half years in the business, he earned seven Million Dollar Club plaques.

But a manager's job is not primarily to sell. It's to help others to sell. And that was what Floyd set out to do.

He believed in doing his share for the company. Once he made the company an offer: "Just give me all the people that are losing and I'll meet with them for a couple of days and show them what to do."

So he came up with a program called "What's the Difference?" in which he tried to pass along the secrets of his and others' sales success. That was before he had even thought of becoming a real estate sales trainer.

In reality, though, he was a trainer for the people in his office and his company.

Lee Real Estate already had a built-in training structure. If you were a new agent, you were assigned to a field trainer until you got nine listings and nine sales. You also had to attend a company-sponsored class every other week for as long you were with the company.

But Floyd went beyond that. He and his agents would have late-night get-togethers during which they would exchange sales tips. But most of the training he gave was one on one, based on his own experience.

This attention to training paid off. His office became the most productive in the company. Then he heard J. Douglas Edwards, he had a new awareness experience, and he moved on to other goals and other commitments.

BRIDGE-BURNING WITH HITLER'S BROTHER

After resolving to pursue a professional speaking career, Floyd gave himself until the end of the year to wind up his career in real estate. In November 1974, he walked into H.B.'s office ready to put a torch to his bridges.

"I'm leaving real estate," Floyd announced.

At the time, his was the top office in the company and he was making a ton of money for himself and for the company.

He was leaving a comfortable and secure home to strike out in the wilderness, and he had none of the survival gear. Had he quit right then and started promoting himself as a speaker, he would have starved. He had no speaking ability. He had nothing. But he believed in commitment; in burning bridges behind him.

So he said to H.B.: "I'm leaving real estate."

H.B. acted as if he were his brother Adolf and Floyd was the general who had just told him, "We're pulling back from Stalingrad, Mein Fuehrer.*"*

"Leaving real estate?" he asked incredulously. "What will you do."

"I thought I'd go into sales training. I listened to Doug Edwards down in Detroit, and I think I can do it."

"You're a damned fool to try. If you're a speaker, I'm a chorus girl."

Floyd took a second look at H.B. He wasn't a chorus girl. Didn't have the legs or the chest.

"Yeah, I know it sounds crazy, H.B., but it's something I want to do. I've run out of challenges in sales and I've run out of challenges in sales management."

"Jeez, Floyd, is it the money? I can raise your commission if that's what you want."

"It's not the money, H.B."

"Tell me what it'll take and I'll try to get it for you."

"It won't take anything, H.B. I've decided I want to go into sales training. It's as simple as that."

Nothing is as simple as that. They went back and forth for about four hours.

Then H.B. asked, "Where are you going to train?"

"Gee, I dunno. I haven't got that far."

"You're standing there telling me you're quitting your job so you can train people, and you don't even know where you're going to train?"

"You gotta make a commitment first," Floyd said. "Then you'll figure out how to get there.

A GRAND A MONTH AND A TITLE

"How would you like to train for this company."

"Great." Floyd had come to set fire to his bridges, not knowing how he'd be earning a living 30 days down the road.

"I'll give you a grand a month," H.B. said.

Now a grand a month, even in 1974, didn't exactly land you in the lap of luxury. In fact, it was a substantial come-down for a person who had managed a real estate office and personally accounted for up to $2 million in sales a year.

Yet Floyd took it. It was a $1,000-a-month raise over what he had lined up otherwise.

Lee Real Estate made him vice president in charge of recruiting and training, and it was a whirlwind one-year experience. Floyd interviewed 800 people for real estate jobs that year. He hired more people in one year than most companies hire forever.

He also got a chance to design programs and to practice in front of the new people. He had an audience that couldn't walk out, which is every speaker's dream. So in that first year, he spoke and recruited and learned, and in general kept too busy to worry about the bridges behind him that were going up in smoke.

His commitment paid off. Just to recap: Here was his process at this point. Awareness came when J. Douglas Edwards said, "Someone out there has greatness in him." Step 2, the goal, came when he typed out, "2,300 people by April 16, 1979." The third step, commitment, came when he told H.B., "I'm leaving."

DON'T GO HALFWAY

When I speak of a commitment, I mean a full-hearted commitment.

A full-hearted commitment is not the same thing as "giving it a try."

When you "give it a try" you're opening yourself to failure. People who say they're going to "give it a try" are psychologically admitting failure at the outset.

To illustrate, try to stand up. Nope, don't stand up. **Try** to stand up. You can't, can you? You're either standing up or you're not. There's no such thing as trying.

When you're sitting on the runway in a 747 and you hear the captain's voice saying, "We're going to try to take off now," I don't care how calm and assured he sounds. Summon the flight attendant and tell her you want off the airplane. You want to fly with a pilot who **knows** he's going to get that sucker off the ground.

In the real estate business, the 70% of the people who drop out before the end of their second year are the people who decided to give it a try. The ones who stay are the ones who made a commitment to succeed.

People are always making half-hearted, conditional commitments.

"I'm going to lose weight as soon as good weather sets in and I can get out and jog."

"I'm going to start a savings account as soon as I get my credit cards paid off."

"I'm going to quit this job as soon as the economy improves and I can find a better one without moving to another city."

If you see somebody who is overweight and broke, and has been stuck in the same old job since the year one, pay close attention: You're looking at a half-hearted commitment.

As Zig Ziglar likes to say, "If you wait to leave home until all the lights are green, you're never going to leave home." If you postpone all the things you want to do until the perfect moment arrives, you'll never do the things you want to do.

I often share with my audiences a poem I learned from Ziglar, and I always get a number of requests for copies. It goes like this:

The bride white of hair stooped over her cane;
Her legs uncertain, need guiding;
And across the church aisle,
With a big toothless smile,
The groom in a wheelchair came riding.

Who is this elderly couple thus wed?
You'll find, if you've closely explored it,
That this is that rare,
Most conservative pair
That waited till they could afford it.

When people make half-hearted commitments, it usually means that they don't believe their goals can be reached. The dreams are no more than fantasies.

As soon as a full-hearted commitment is made, the belief in oneself becomes automatic. And once you believe in yourself, your subconscious begins guiding your behavior in a way that will bring about the fulfillment of your commitment.

COMMITMENT WILL SEE YOU THROUGH

There have been moments in Floyd's career when anything less than a full-hearted commitment would have doomed him to the ash heap of history.

One of them came during his third year as a speaker. He had been flying high. In the first year he had earned about $260,000. In the second year he did better than that. In the third year he went into Chapter 11 bankruptcy. The reason: He had expanded too far too fast and had lost control.

One afternoon he was sitting in his lawyer's office and they were going over the options.

"What are you going to do now?" the lawyer asked.

Floyd was shocked that he would ask. The attorney was talking to a committed man. Floyd told him: "I'm going to meet all of my debts, dollar for dollar, regardless of what the court tells me I have to do. And then I'm going to continue to work on my goal of being the creator of the number-one sales-training organization in North America."

The lawyer may have thought Floyd was in need of another kind of commitment—the kind that calls for strong men in white coats carrying a strait jacket. But his commitment saw him through. The next year he earned about $1.2 million. Each year got progressively better. He's still committed. And his credit's good.

VERBALIZE YOUR COMMITMENT

So how do you go about making that full-hearted commitment?

We've already established that you first have to achieve awareness, and then you have to set a goal.

The next step is to verbalize your commitment to the goal. One way is to rent a blimp encrusted with neon letters that read "I'm going to lose 40 pounds, make a million bucks and retire to Tahiti." If that's impractical, find some other way to spread the word around to your friends and acquaintances.

Don't worry about those who may accuse you of bragging. As Dizzy Dean, Arkansas' most famous philosopher, used to say, "It ain't braggin' if you can do it."

INVOLVE YOUR FAMILY

Next, bring your family into the picture. If you're married, you might start by taking your spouse to a pizzeria at Van Dyke and Lynch, ordering an Italian meal and some wine, and saying, "Honey, I've decided to go to the top and I want you to come along with me."

Help your spouse to understand your goal and how it will help the family cause. I wanted to assure Linda that achieving my goal would not diminish my love for her or rob us of time together. She knows now that if my schedule begins to starve our relationship, all she has to do is say, "Come home Floyd." And I'll come running.

This kind of assurance has meant that Linda is willing to reinforce my commitment with a commitment of her own. It can work that way with your spouse.

Fulfilling a commitment may mean that you have fewer hours to spend with your family. But when it comes to family time, quality is more important than quantity. If that were not true, the ideal parent would be the unemployed bum who spends all his time at home watching television and swigging beer.

If you check the divorce courts, you'll find that families with breadwinners working 40-hour weeks split just as often as those in which the breadwinner works 60-hour weeks. The difference is in how you spend the time. Do you take the time to talk to the kids, check on their school progress, offer help with their homework? Do you and your spouse occasionally do the candlelight and wine bit? Do you talk over mutual problems and listen to each other?

If you do, then your commitment to your goals should not weaken your relationship.

MAKE AN INVESTMENT

A wholehearted commitment calls for investment. This investment could take the form of a learning program or a training course. It could mean spending money on tools, supplies and office space.

I've known salespeople who dawdled in mediocrity because they were unwilling to make that investment.

"So what's your goal, Joe?"

"Oh, I'm gonna buy a new car soon as I start making enough money."

"Yeah? What kind?"

"Maybe a Ford Taurus. Yeah, that's a nice car."

"When you gonna get it?"

"Whenever I start making the money."

"There's a Ford dealership down the street, Joe. Show me the Taurus you're going to buy."

The truth is, Joe is never going to earn the money for that Taurus until he is willing to make an investment in his commitment.

But let me take him down to the lot, turn him over to a skillful salesman, and get him to sign an installment contract. Joe will drive that Taurus home, and he won't miss a payment. Why? That installment note was the investment he needed to make his commitment a wholehearted one.

KEEP A QUARTER HANDY

That brings me to Shamus McPherson, a frugal sort who spent a lot of time at a neighborhood tavern in Detroit.

Shamus never turned down a free drink, and if push came to shove he'd even buy his own, though Shamus would go to great lengths to keep push from coming to shove.

One night, as was his custom, Shamus fell in with a crowd of hearty companions who were taking turns buying rounds for the whole group. Shamus positioned himself at the end of the line, and by the time it came his turn he arranged to be in the men's room clearing the way for a few more rounds. Having completed this ritual, Shamus looked down and was dismayed to see that he had dropped a dime into the bowl.

Shamus now faced a cruel dilemma. Should he flush the dime into the Detroit River? Or should he contaminate his hands by reaching into the bowl to rescue it?

He stood and agonized over the decision.

Finally, he decided that a mere dime was not worth the contamination.

So he threw in a quarter, then reached in and retrieved both coins.

Shamus made a commitment, and he made an investment that sealed the commitment.

So dare to dream. Set your goals. Make your commitment. And keep a quarter handy.

NO EMPTY PROMISES

Remember that a commitment is not an empty promise to yourself. It's a promise with teeth in it. It's like Caesar crossing the Rubicon: Once he crossed that river, there was no turning back. He had to go to Rome and he had to stake his claim to authority.

The best way to make your commitment stick is to burn your bridges. When you decide to move on to something else, close the door behind you, lock it and throw away the key.

Make it a whole-hearted commitment; leave yourself no excuses for failure. Then make your commitment public. By telling everyone what you plan to do, you challenge yourself through positive stress. Your friends will cheer you on, giving you the inspiration and the energy to attain your goal. Your enemies will be waiting for you to fall on your face. This will give you the incentive to show them how wrong they are.

Verbalize your commitment. Put it in writing.

Involve your family. Let them know what you plan to do, and let them be a part of it.

Then make an investment. When you've invested in your commitment you have a strong reason to stick with it until you've reached your goal.

List the most important points you have gained from the preceding Step:

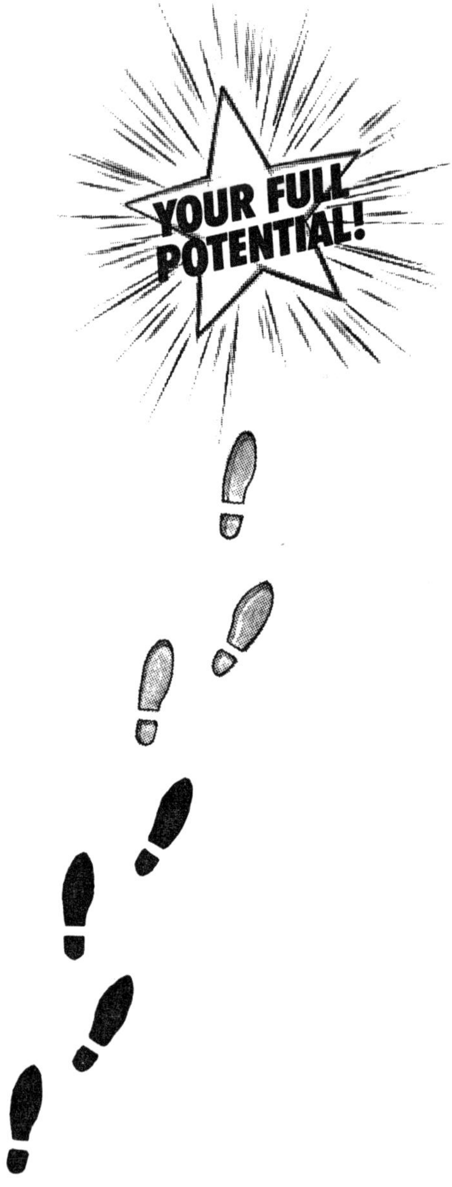
YOUR FULL POTENTIAL!

Step Four

Work Hard and Work Smart

A commitment is no good unless you carry it out. Carrying it out involves a four-letter word that many people regard as obscene. That word is "WORK."

Let's be clear on this: Working hard, by itself, will not do it. Working smart, by itself, will not do it. You've got to learn to work both hard and smart. It's Step Four on the road to greatness, and it's a logical follow-up to the first three steps.

Awareness is "can do."
Goal-setting is "want to."
Commitment is "have to."
Work is "doing."

MAKE THE EXTRA EFFORT

A little extra effort can take you a long way down the road to greatness. Today, working hard means going to work at 8 A.M., working until noon, eating lunch for an hour and working until 5 P.M.

I don't know whether it's unions, soft employees or soft employers, but people have convinced themselves that this is working hard.

Okay, let me offer you a challenge: Start work at 7 A.M., not 8 A.M. Stop work at 9 P.M., not 5 P.M. Work at least half a day every Saturday. Do it for a month. Then ask yourself whether you are less healthy than you were 30 days earlier.

I've tried it for many years, and the answer for me is, "No." With that kind of schedule, I actually feel healthier and more motivated than I felt in those youthful years when 5 o'clock was Miller Time.

JAKE AND THE RICH MAN

In a small Virginia town, there lived a street cleaner named Jake who was paid by the city to be out bright and early to sweep up last night's garbage before today's garbage hit the streets.

Each morning at a quarter to six he would encounter the town's richest citizen—a man who had made his fortune in the peanut business (Jimmy Carter isn't the only one who can do it). We'll call him Mr. Planter.

As Mr. Planter made his way to his office, he always gave Jake a friendly greeting. One morning, Jake asked him:

"Mr. Planter, why does a millionaire like you get up and go to work at 6 o'clock in the morning?"

"That's how I got to be a millionaire," answered Mr. Planter.

The millionaire businessman was at work long after Jake the street cleaner had put away his broom and basket too. Hard work does not guarantee success, but it is the price of success, and not everybody is willing to pay the price.

PLUNGE RIGHT IN

Getting started is one of the hardest things about hard work. We just don't want to get up in the morning, and after we get up we just don't want to get down to work. How much time is wasted around your average office because the staff has to come in, pour the coffee, read the sports pages and work the crosswords before getting down to the hard work of the enterprise?

But getting started is not that bad. You know what it's like to go swimming in a cool body of water. If you wade in gradually, every part of your body takes turns shivering. You prolong the agony. If you plunge right in, the shock is over in a moment and you start enjoying the refreshing coolness. Plunge right into the beginning of your work and see how comfortably the rest of it flows.

TAKE ADVANTAGE OF TIME AND CIRCUMSTANCES

If you want to accomplish something over and above the ordinary, you're going to have to work over and above the ordinary.

Always be alert for opportunities to make that extra effort, even when the circumstances seem unfavorable. I know of a guy who put in some extra time over and above what was required of him, and he got rich in the process. He wasn't working for a Fortune 500 company. He was serving time in a penitentiary.

This guy could have spent his time making license plates or working in the prison laundry and collecting his good time toward early release.

But he decided to make his time count. He noticed that a lot of the guards and convicts preferred custom-fitted uniforms. He had been a tailor on the outside. So he offered to tailor their uniforms—for a fee.

After 20 years of this, he accumulated a fortune. When his sentence was up, he was able to prosper without returning to a life of crime.

How did he do it?

"Instead of serving time, I had time serve me," he said. He could do it because he wasn't afraid of work.

I know that in sales, the business goes to the salespeople who work for it.

This means working hard and working smart. It calls for cold prospecting, which is something too many salespeople hate. But the ones who get ahead are the ones who take down their city directories and start working their way through the addresses and telephone numbers, looking for that one person in a crowd of prospects who might be interested in or have a need for the product being sold. The agents who get ahead are the ones who pound the pavement getting to know their potential customers, who keep in touch with them through regular newsletters and other devices.

That's work, and it can be discouraging and boring. But you have to do that before you experience the excitement of a major deal closed, a Salesperson of the Month award, a Million Dollar Club plaque.

WORK SMART

As I said earlier, hard work alone doesn't ensure success. It has to be smart work as well. The farmer who goes out and plows under a field of weeds has done a lot of work, but he has accomplished nothing unless he goes back and applies fertilizer, plants seed, controls the weeds and, finally, harvests the crop.

A bricklayer's labor is in vain if he builds half a wall, then goes off somewhere else to build half of another wall. Projects have to be completed.

A salesperson who lets a call end with "let me think about it for a few days, then call me back" has left a project uncompleted. What happens to farmers who plow their fields, then let them lie for a couple of months? They find that the weeds have reclaimed their territory and they'll have to plow the fields all over. So finish what you start.

SET PRIORITIES

Working smart also means working on the right things in the right order.

Suppose you go to a doctor and say, "Hey doc, I've got an ingrown toenail and, oh by the way, I think I also just severed an artery."

The doctor isn't going to say, "Okay, I'll take care of the toenail first, then we'll see about that artery." He has to establish his priorities, and if he doesn't patch the artery first he can forget about repeat business.

In business, it's surprising how often people worry about ingrown toenails when they ought to be thinking about the bleeding arteries.

Time is money, and when you waste time on low-priority, nonproductive things, money is flowing out of your business like blood out of an open artery.

On occasion, I ask people in my company to list all the unaccomplished tasks they're working on. Then I ask them to mark off every task they don't really have to work on. They usually discover that from 30% to 50% of the things they do don't really have to be done.

To work smart, make a list of the things you **need** to do. Then list them in the order of importance. Think about the end result you're looking for, the degree to which each item on your list will contribute toward the end result, and how long it's going to take you to carry out each task. Your first priority should be the item that will take you the farthest toward your goal in the shortest time.

You may start the day with 10 items on your list and be able to complete only two of them.

That's okay. Next day, make another list of 10 items, rank them in order of importance, and again take them one at a time.

If you do this every day, you'll soon be in the top 10% of achievers. Do it for 30 days and you'll be well on your way to changing your life for the better.

FILL THE VOID

If you keep a careful log of your time, you'll be amazed at how much of it you spend doing nothing productive.

How much time do you spend driving to work? Do you spend it cursing other drivers or listening to the mindless chatter of a disc jockey?

You can make that time count toward your goal. No matter what that goal is, there are cassette albums out there that will give you valuable tips on reaching it. You don't have a cassette deck in your car? Spend $150 and get one.

So you spend $75 for a three-hour seminar on selling real estate. I can spend $75 for a cassette album on the same subject (possibly by the same speaker). I listen to it in my car stereo. I continue to play it at my office, all the while I am making calls that will make me money. It isn't that your time is wasted at the seminar (especially if it's one of mine). It's just that you're using it more efficiently by making your calls while you're listening to the tapes (especially if they're my tapes).

What do you do between the time you get home from work and the time you go to bed? Do you spend it in that vast wasteland known as prime-time television?

Sure there are some worthwhile programs on the tube. Some of them may even help you become a better-informed, more well-rounded person. But face it, much of what you see is like the Styrofoam popcorn used in packing things: It's just there to fill up space in your schedule. Spend that time on activities that will move you toward your goal.

What other idle time could you use better?

Some business people take little note pads with them wherever they go—to the bedside, to the beach, to lunch, to dinner. Then, whenever profitable ideas occur, they write them down, to be followed up at appropriate times.

That doesn't mean that you stay on the job 24 hours a day. A balanced individual has to take time for relaxation, recreation, and constructive activities that don't necessarily involve the job. But within your workday itself, you'll find many opportunities to fill void time with pay time.

LEARN TO SAY NO

If you're one of the good guys, you like to help other people, which is great. In fact, helping others is one of the secrets to success, and we're going to devote a whole chapter to it.

But there is such a thing as being too helpful. Sometimes we allow people to rely too heavily on us, to the extent that they fail to carry their own loads. They shift their burdens onto us, and we become so entangled with their activities that we neglect our own.

Therefore, one of the secrets to working effectively is learning to say "no."

It helps if you have your own priorities straight. Suppose Marvin says, "Hey Floyd, I'm going to watch the Pistons play the Bulls. Could you show a house for me at four?"

Now it happens that I have a 5 o'clock appointment to show a house to this couple who are relocating from Toledo. If I do Marvin this favor, I may be late for my appointment, and it could cost me a sale. Besides, I had planned to do some prospecting by telephone between the showing and 9 P.M.

Is good old Floyd going to say, "Okay, Marvin; I have my own appointment at five, and then I was going to prospect, but I'll try to squeeze you in"?

Not if Floyd plans to make the Million Dollar Club this year.

It's up to Marvin to work his calendar around the Pistons' schedule. That's not Floyd's responsibility.

Now suppose Marvin were to come to me and say, "Floyd, I just got a phone call from the hospital. My mother has just been admitted with a massive heart attack. I'm due to show a house at 4 this afternoon. Can you stand in for me?"

That would be a different matter. I'd tell Marvin to go check on his mother and I'd take care of his appointment.

Maybe I would squeeze it into my schedule. Maybe I would find another salesperson who could handle it more conveniently. Or maybe I would call the prospects, explain the situation, and set up another appointment. In any case, I'd find some way to take the pressure off Marvin.

Of course, knowing Marvin, I might call the hospital to find out if his mother really **had** been admitted with a massive heart attack; then I'd check the Pistons' schedule and call the airport to see whether he was booked on the next flight to Chicago. Just kidding.

Real estate isn't the only area in which we sometimes let people shove their work off on us. Many mothers devote their lives to waiting on their children, cleaning their rooms, picking up their clothes, taking care of the dishes. They're doing them no favors. The wise mother will teach her children to do things for themselves. This gives her more time to devote to her own personal goals. And it equips the children to make their own ways in life when they are out from under mother's wing.

When you're inclined to do favors for people, ask yourself whether what you're about to do is really a favor. When you encourage

Marvin to put his customers second to the Detroit Pistons, you're doing him no favors, and you're certainly not helping yourself.

OVERCOME THE OBSTACLES

No one can be successful—in sales or in any other pursuit—without learning how to overcome obstacles. For a salesperson, this may be three or four sales falling through. For a doctor it may be a patient with symptoms that refuse to yield to conventional treatment. For a lawyer it may be a case in which the facts are so complex and convoluted that no ordinary jury can understand them. For a ski-resort owner, it may be a season in which December-through-February temperatures average 60 degrees under fair skies.

Obstacles such as these can throw some people into depression and rob them of the energy they need to succeed.

There's a way around most obstacles. Often it means going back to the basics.

For the salesperson, it may mean forgetting the sales that fell through and concentrating on new business. It may mean making those prospecting calls and getting face to face with the people. For the doctor, it may mean spending some extra time researching medical books and articles, or perhaps consulting with a colleague with experience in ailments of that sort. For the lawyer, it may be using charts and other visual aids to make the complex simple. For the ski-resort owner, it may mean investing in some snow-making equipment or finding some warm-weather recreational activities that will bring people to the lodge when there's no snow on the slopes.

Whatever the situation, don't let it obscure your goal.

Some obstacles just have to be ignored. If you're running a golf shop and it rains for 40 days and 40 nights, it's going to hurt your business and there's nothing you can do about it. You can spend your days staring out the window and bemoaning your misfortune. Or you can spend your time planning ways to increase your profits when the sun shines again—as it always does. If worst comes to worst, you can go into the ark-building business.

Obstacles will flatten you only if you let them. Stephen Hawking encountered a normally crippling obstacle just as he was *beginning a promising career as a physicist.* While he was still in his 20s, he came down with amyotrophic lateral sclerosis, an incurable disease of the neurological system that progressively disables the victim. The disease left him almost totally incapacitated physically. He can't walk, he can't dress, he can't wait on himself. What can he do?

He can explore the universe through the power of the mind. Stephen Hawking has one of the most comprehensive understandings of the universe of any man alive. He combined Einstein's theory of relativity with the theory of quantum mechanics to propound the theory of exploding black holes. He has told us about things many people thought it was impossible to learn about. He became one of the youngest people ever elected to Britain's Royal Society, and went on to hold the professorship at Cambridge University once held by Sir Isaac Newton.

How did he do all this?

He worked hard with what he had, which was an incredibly brilliant mind, an enormous fund of courage—and little else.

I personally encountered a young man in Indianapolis with a handicap that would have had most people throwing in the towel before the bell for Round One.

This young man is a very successful salesperson. He didn't succeed through a lot of fancy leg work; he has only one leg. He didn't succeed through a glib tongue; half his tongue is missing.

He did it by ignoring the obstacles and focusing on the assets he did have—courage, ingenuity, and a winning personality.

"How did you manage to succeed with obstacles like that?" I asked him.

"Well, there's nothing I can do about it," he said. "It's already happened. So I might as well make the best of what I have."

Obstacles have a way of melting before people who are willing to work. They're like boulders that try to stop a river from following its course. When a landslide throws huge rocks into the stream, the river just swirls around them and over them. Eventually the boulders are worn away or just become a part of the scenery. The river keeps rolling toward the sea. When somebody throws a dam across its path, the river patiently gathers its waters until they're high enough to get over the dam. And it rolls placidly toward the sea. When a mountain stands in the way, the river curves around its base until it finds a way around it. Whatever the obstacle, there's always a way to deal with it.

For some people, of course, the principal obstacle to success is work. If you regard it as a four-letter obscenity, you have three options:

1. Redefine the word.
2. Learn to live with the obscenity.
3. Or resign yourself to failure.

By far, the best option is to redefine the word. That's what a young recruit named Wickman did in Navy boot camp when he was asked to wash out the GI cans. His new definition of work was this: "A game that combines fun and accomplishment."

AVOIDING THE THREE EVILS

Voltaire, a French guy who said a lot of smart things, maintained that "Work keeps us from three evils: boredom, vice and need."

I'm living proof of that. Why did I do all those dumb things when I was catting around on the streets of Detroit?

Because I was bored. I didn't have anything productive to fill my idle hours, so I filled them with foolish things: joy-riding, chasing chicks, getting high.

Why couldn't I provide my family with a decent living during my Navy years, my milk-route years and my bar tending years?

Because I wasn't working at success. I did what was expected—sometimes a tad more than was expected, but never much more than was required. So I was bored, turned to vice, and found myself in need. The Frenchman was right.

I avoided hard work because I had not been clued in on an important truth: Work can bring you a great deal of pleasure.

As the writer of Ecclesiastes put it: "There is nothing better for a man than that he should eat and drink and make his soul enjoy good in his labor."

The unsuccessful people are the ones who don't make it past the eating and drinking. They stop before they get to the word "labor," which is a five-letter synonym for "work." Pretty soon, they find that they can't afford the eating and drinking.

"Work fascinates me," said the penniless hobo. "I can sit and watch it all day."

That's a good philosophy of life, if you're content to be a hobo.

Too many people try to follow the ABC's of success. They ask for it, they beg for it, they cry for it, when often the answer is all the way down the alphabet to the W: Work for it.

Most of us like the finer things of life, and those of us who lacked the foresight to be born to wealth have to work to achieve them.

TAKE OUT THE DRUDGERY

But that's no tragedy. Work should not be identified with mindless drudgery. Michelangelo worked hard, and the painting on the ceiling of the Cistine Chapel was the result. Do you think he regarded that as drudgery?

Leonardo worked hard and produced the Mona Lisa. Thomas

Jefferson worked hard and produced the Declaration of Independence. Samuel Morse worked hard and produced the telegraph. Thomas Edison worked hard and produced the light bulb. Thomas Watson worked hard and produced IBM.

What was the difference between their work and the work of the toiling peasant, the factory slave and the assembly-line robot?

They were working toward their own goals. They were doing the things they were good at doing; the things they liked to do.

Thomas Edison had dreams, but he knew that those dreams would not fulfill themselves.

"There's no substitute for hard work," he said. Sure, Edison was a genius, but what was his definition of genius? "One percent inspiration and 99% perspiration."

THE GREAT EQUALIZER

Sir William Osler, the Canadian physician and medical professor, called work "the open sesame to every portal, the great equalizer in the world, the true philosopher's stone which transmutes all the base metal of humanity into gold." If I could use words like that, they'd call me "Sir Floyd" and name a disease after me too.

"The great equalizer." That's a good point. Floyd Wickman never claimed to be a great genius. But I am a great worker. That willingness to work gives me a head start. I know lots of people smarter than I am who are still paycheck slaves because they're not willing to put out the extra effort required to succeed.

There's some drudgery in every line of work. Artists have to mix their paints and clean their brushes. Authors have to type their manuscripts and correct their errors. Few Pulitzer Prize-winning journalists reached the top without writing obits, covering Planning Commission meetings and writing puff pieces for the Blood Bank and the United Way. Singers and musicians have to practice, practice, practice.

But they perform this drudgery because it's the "open sesame" to the rewards of their crafts.

"I don't like work," said Joseph Conrad, the Russian-born English novelist; "No man does—but I like what is in work—the chance to find yourself."

LET YOUR DREAMS STIMULATE YOU

Adds historian and essayist Thomas Carlyle: "All work is as seed sown; it grows and spreads and sows itself anew."

If the work you do isn't offering you this chance to find yourself; if its seeds aren't growing, spreading and sowing themselves anew, maybe it's time to open up your awareness and do a little dreaming.

As Walter Pater, a British essayist and critic, put it: "We need some imaginative stimulus, some not impossible ideal such as may shape vague hope and transform it into effective desire, to carry us year after year, without disgust, through the routine work which is so large a part of life."[1]

I think the guy was saying that we need to find the type of work that stimulates the imagination. It may be programming a computer, plowing a field, or laying bricks. All of these jobs sound boring to a lot of people, but to others they're pathways to fulfillment. You're familiar with the three men working with bricks and mortar and trowels who were asked, "What are you doing?"

The first one said, "I'm laying bricks."

The second said, "I'm building a wall."

The third one said, "I'm creating a beautiful cathedral."

The third one is the one who gets fulfillment from his work. By the way, he's also the one a critic would say is crazy.

---

[1]Walter Pater, Marius the Epicurean, (1885) Chapter 25.

FULFILLMENT ON THE FARM

A city slicker once asked a successful farmer what it took to get ahead on the farm.

"Hard work," he said.

"I work hard too," the city guy told him. "Tell me how your day goes."

"Well, the first thing I do is milk 100 cows. Then I feed them, feed the chickens and gather the eggs.

"After that, I slop the hogs and make the rounds of the farm, looking for any fences that need mending. Then I get on my tractor and go out and plow about 10 acres."

"That sounds like a heavy schedule," admitted the city fellow. "What do you do when you've finished your plowing?"

"I eat breakfast," said the farmer.

What does it take to keep a farmer toiling away day after day, when there's no boss looking over his shoulder, no time clock to punch, no class waiting for him to teach, no audience waiting for him to speak?

Let's review once more his steps for achieving his full potential:

Step 1. He has awareness. He can see the fertile fields out there, full of weeds at the moment maybe, but full of potential for corn and wheat and soybeans.

Step 2. He has a goal: A bumper harvest from each crop. Two hundred bushels to the acre of corn. So many gallons of milk from his cows. So many pounds of butterfat for the dairy.

Step 3. He has a commitment: If the crop doesn't come in, the mortgage doesn't get paid, the bank gets the land and the family gets no Christmas. He burns his bridges every season. But he makes a full-hearted commitment to bring in the crop, and he makes a solid investment in money, time and. . . .

Step 4. Work. The work the farmer does fulfills the criteria laid down by W. E. B. DuBois, the great black reformer, on the occasion of his 90th birthday in 1958:

"The return from your work must be the satisfaction which that work brings you and the world's need of that work. With this, life is heaven, or as near heaven as you can get. Without this—with work which you despise, which bores you, and which the world does not need—this life is hell."

JOE PATERNO AND HIS HYPOTENUSES

You think there are jobs in which it's all play and no work? How about a coaching football? Now that's an exciting occupation. No drudgery there—it's always "Rah! Rah! and "Win one for the Gipper."

Let me tell you about Joe Paterno and how he developed the two-deep zone defense.

In his first year as head coach at Penn State, Paterno's team had all the excitement of an algebra test. Joe knew he had to do something if he was to fulfill his goal of becoming the greatest coach in football history.

One of his problems was that he didn't have a great team, especially when it came to defense. As he put it, "I had to find a way of playing great defense without great defensive athletes."[2]

So Paterno holed up in a small room in his home. He figured out a way to overcome his defensive weakness. Instead of playing a seven-man line, he'd put an eighth man up front.

But that would leave him with only three pass defenders. What would he do if the opposing team sent out four potential receivers?

Paterno went to work with pencil and pad. He wore out several erasers. But after several weeks, he came up with what was then a

---

[2]Joe Paterno with Bernard Asbell, Paterno: By the Book New York: Random House, Inc., 1989), p. 96.

novel defense. He deployed his three pass receivers so that no matter where the quarterback threw the ball, one of them could get to the receiver in time. He used the same principles employed in baseball, when the left fielder covers for the centerfielder when the centerfielder is shifted toward right for a left-handed pull hitter. Sound like fun?

The way Paterno tells it sounds more like work:

> "After working out the principles of the plays, I had to figure lengths of hypotenuses between sides of triangles and whatnot to develop mathematical rules of where to place those men in the secondary. If the quarterback got the ball on the left hash, and if the guy you assume is the receiver is X yards from him and will be able to run 6 yards deep, I had to figure out just where my 'left fielder' had to be, if he was of equal speed, to meet the intended receiver at 20 yards deep and prevent a completion. Then I figured out that the 'center fielder' had to be as distant horizontally from the 'left fielder' as the 'left fielder' was down field from the potential receiver, and so forth."[3]

Lengths of hypotenuses? I thought a hypotenuse was an African animal that grows to the approximate size of Refrigerator Perry. While I was hanging around Audrey's house during school hours or catting around on the streets of Detroit, Paterno was learning that a hypotenuse is a line on a triangle, and if you know how long it is you can tell how long the other lines are. If Mr. Holt had told me that, I might have said, "Okay, but how is that going to make me any happier or more successful?"

It made Joe Paterno a lot happier and a lot more successful. It helped him determine where to place those pass defenders. That in turn helped him bring in a whole new era of football success at Penn State. It took some hard mental work to learn the difference between a hypotenuse and a hippopotamus, and some more hard

[3]Ibid. p. 102.

work to figure out the connection between a hypotenuse and a half-back. Paterno undoubtedly would have had more fun at the swimming pool, or wading in a trout stream or maybe putting around on the golf course. But his hard work paid off in winning football teams at Penn State. Paterno probably had lots of fun on those post-season trips to New Orleans, and he probably has gotten a lot of enjoyment out of all the nice things a big-time coach's salary can buy these days.

So if you want to achieve greatness, put some action into your commitment. Go to work. Find opportunities to exert that extra effort that propels you down the road to success. But make sure that extra effort isn't wasted on wheel-spinning. Work smart. Set your priorities. Take advantage of time and circumstances. Look for empty spaces in your schedule—blocks of time in which you're doing nothing constructive. Find ways to fill those voids with activities that take you toward your goal. When you encounter obstacles, look for ways to overcome them. Go back to the basics. Put hard work and ingenuity to work. If the obstacles can't be overcome, find ways to go around them.

Look for ways to take the drudgery out of your work. Work is seldom a drudge when it's being applied toward your own goals. Set a goal that you really want to achieve, then work toward it. You'll find the work to be fulfilling instead of boring.

And remember, work is what keeps you from those three evils: boredom, vice and need.

When you've learned the value of working hard and working smart, you're ready for Step Five on the road to achievement of your full potential. Stick with me. We're almost there.

List the most important points you have gained from the preceding Step:

YOUR FULL POTENTIAL!

Step Five

Give Unselfishly in Order to Get

Successful people give. They don't give because they're successful; they're successful because they give. They don't give in the expectation that giving will make them rich. They give out of a spirit of generosity. They don't give for publicity or applause. They give in secret. If you expect to achieve your full potential, you too need to learn the truth of the saying that has become the corporate motto of my company: "We get by giving."

To whom do successful people give?

They may give their time, money and expertise to some worthy organization. Or they may look for individuals in need of help.

Giving indiscriminately doesn't do the job. For instance, if you give money unconditionally to people whom you know to be alcoholics or drug addicts, you're not helping the individuals. You're subsidizing their destructive behavior. The effective giver is the one who finds someone who can use the gift as a springboard to success. In his book, The Platinum Rule, fellow Michigander Art Fettig recommends that you find someone with a special need. This is usually a temporary need, one that can be taken care of with a single act of assistance. It should be a need that can be taken care of through the application of your talents and your abilities.

Fettig uses an illustration: Suppose you have a locomotive with a long train of cars, all of them heavily loaded. To start that train to moving requires a tremendous amount of power. But after the train is under way, it takes only a fraction of that power to keep it moving.

The locomotive has only 97% of the power required to start the load to rolling. If another locomotive could ease up behind and give it a push, the first locomotive could haul the load to its destination unassisted.

As an ex-Navy man, I can think of another illustration. One of the bravest things a military man is required to do on a routine basis is to take off in a jet aircraft from the deck of a carrier. In the Navy they say that you've got to be a little crazy to get into an airplane with a bomb on one end and a fire on the other and let them throw you off of a perfectly good ship in the middle of the ocean. But those guys do it, and it's an awesome sight to see an F-14 Tomcat roar down that flight deck and climb over the ocean, its twin tailpipes glowing like peepholes into hell.

But if that Tomcat depended solely on its own engines, its destination might be the deep blue under instead of the wild blue yonder. It might never make it aloft on its own power. To give the extra boost to get the fighter airborne, the carrier has catapults that accelerate the airplanes to take-off speed. After that, the Tomcat will achieve, on its own, speeds several times the speed of sound. But it needs that boost.

So you're looking for people for whom you can provide that little extra boost to get them airborne.

SKIP THE FANFARE

Once you've found a person you can help, do you call up the newspapers and TV stations and hire a photographer to record the boost you're going to give?

No. If you do, it doesn't count. In fact, it's best if you require that the people you're going to assist take vows of secrecy.

They must never reveal to anyone else that you've given them a hand. And you have to promise the same thing: You're not going to tell anyone what you did.

"Take heed that ye do not your righteousness before men to be seen of them," wrote the great teacher of Nazareth. "else ye have no reward with your father who is in heaven." Instead, "Let not thy left hand know what thy right hand doeth: that thine alms may be in secret; and thy father who seeth in secret shall recompense thee."

When you do this, good things start to happen.

A GOOD DEED ON THE ROAD

It was about three years after Floyd had vowed to go to the top in real estate. Things were going well, but not great. He was working his buns off getting listings, and was making good progress on sales, but something was missing. He wasn't getting any referrals. Now referrals are supposed to be the gravy ladled out by your satisfied customers. But Floyd wasn't getting any.

One day, he was driving north on the freeway, headed home, when he spotted a disabled car in the southbound lane. A black woman was standing beside it. Several children were with her.

It was almost a mile to the next exit, but Floyd took it and went back to that disabled car.

"What seems to be the trouble?" he asked.

She pointed to her rear tire. Floyd had seen pancakes that weren't that flat.

"Well, that won't be much of a problem," he said. "Do you have a jack?"

"Yes sir, but my spare is flat," she said.

The kids were all looking at Floyd expectantly now. Would he say, "Well, I'm sorry, there's nothing I can do for you," and drive away?

Floyd couldn't do that.

SANTA CLAUS IN A BUICK

"We'll put the spare in my car and find a service station that will fix it," he told her.

Floyd could see her hesitancy, and he knew that it wasn't just fear of getting into a car with a strange white man.

"It's okay," he said. "I'll see to it that your tire gets fixed and you and the kids can be on your way." Something about the way he spoke must have reassured her.

Floyd threw the spare into his trunk and opened the back door. The kids piled in. They drove to a reputable-looking service station and Floyd took the spare to the attendant. The tread had seen better days, but the carcass looked sound.

"Do you suppose you can fix this tire for this lady and put it back on her car?"

"Where's her car?"

"It's a couple of miles south on the freeway."

"It's gonna be five bucks to fix the flat and ten to put it back on her car."

Floyd handed him a twenty.

"This should take care of it," he said. "I want the tire fixed and the lady and her kids safely on their way."

Then he went back to the car.

"They're going to take care of you here," he said. "They'll fix your tire and take you back to the car and put it on for you."

"I don't have any money to pay them," said the woman.

"You don't need any money," Floyd told her. "It's all been taken care of."

The woman and the kids must have thought Santa Claus had just come rolling down the freeway in a Buick LeSabre.

Floyd went home that night feeling extremely good about what he had done.

He could have said to the woman, "I'm Floyd Wickman, and I'm with Lee Real Estate. Here's my card. If you ever decide to sell your house get in touch."

But he didn't. He didn't tell her who he was or what he did for a living. He just told the guy to fix her tire and he gave him the money to do it.

Floyd didn't do that good deed out of any selfish motive, and he didn't go around bragging about it to everybody who would listen.

But from that week on, when he began doing things unselfishly for other people, the referral situation changed. He began getting calls from people who would say, "You sold a house for my brother-in-law and I want you to sell mine."

His customers started telling other people about him. Floyd was amazed. Did Floyd believe one thing had to do with the other? Yes. Did it? Who really knows or could prove it if it did?

DON'T COUNT THE COST

When you decide to give, don't count the cost. Lots of people have trouble with that idea.

"I'd love to give, but I've barely enough for myself to keep soul and body together," some say.

Perhaps they should learn the meaning of the prayer uttered by St. Ignatius of Loyola: "Teach us, good Lord . . . to give and not to count the cost."

If you check most wealthy philanthropists, you'll find that they were philanthropists before they were wealthy.

In fact, you'll be amazed at the people who will tell you they began to prosper only after they developed the habit of giving.

"He who soweth sparingly shall reap also sparingly," said Paul, "and he that soweth bountifully shall reap also bountifully."

At first glance, this may seem to make no mathematical or logical sense at all. How can you acquire wealth by giving things away?

Philosophers can debate why this happens. It could be that the good deeds we do are like seeds sown by a farmer. If a farmer wants a bountiful wheat crop, he must sow a lot of wheat seeds. If we want good things to come to us, we have to sow good things.

Perhaps there's a benevolent force in the universe that is guided by good deeds; that arranges events so that a good deed performed is a good deed rewarded.

Perhaps it's just that good deeds nourish the self-esteem in our subconscious minds, and our subconscious minds in turn cultivate the habits and practices that lead to success. Or maybe the good deeds we do inspire the people with whom we interact to good deeds, and when you're in a crowd of people who are doing good deeds, some of those good deeds are going to be done to you.

How should I know? I'm just an ex-street kid from the east side of Detroit.

HOW DO I LOVE THEE

A book by Og Mandino entitled The Greatest Salesman in the World helped Floyd get a balanced understanding of the meaning and power of love.

It was an unusual book about a Middle Easterner named Omar who owned a market. One day Omar discovered some scrolls in a chest. These scrolls unlocked for Omar the secrets of life.

One of them dealt with love.

Now love was not a subject that came up very often on the streets of Detroit's east side. Even when you were going steady with a girl, you didn't say you ''loved'' her. You said you ''liked'' her. Love was for softies and cats were tough guys.

Love isn't a word you hear very often in a real estate office either. Somehow it doesn't come up much in the context of adjustable-rate mortgages, bank appraisals, multiple listings and cold-call prospecting.

But Mandino's book introduced Floyd to the concept of love.

When Elizabeth Barrett Browning was writing poetry to gruff old George, she wrote:

> *How do I love thee?*
> *Let me count the ways. . . .''*

Then she went on to say a lot of mushy stuff that Floyd Wickman would never say because he just doesn't talk or write like that.

You're not going to see Floyd going up to some burly house-hunter with a thick beard and smelly pipe and say to him, ''I love thee to the breadth and depth and height my soul can reach when feeling out of sight. . . .''

Even if he said that to Linda, she'd look at him kind of funny and ask what he'd been drinking.

The Greeks have a better way of talking about love. They have several different words for it.

When a young guy sees a Greek goddess walking among the flowers and has a yearning to hold her in his embrace, the Greeks say he is smitten by eros. That's probably the way Eliza-

beth felt about George, and it's the way Floyd has felt about Linda since the first time he bummed a match from her.

When a Greek man says he loves his children and grandchildren, he's talking about "storge"—family love.

When he embraces his long-lost lodge brother, he's feeling "philia," or brotherly love. Philia is the way the people in Philadelphia feel about the Phillies when they're winning.

THE NOBLEST LOVE OF ALL

But the noblest love of all to the Greek is agape. That's the love that's usually spoken of in the Christian writings in the Bible, most of which were originally written in Greek.

Agape is the word for the principled love that we should have for all mankind. It's the word that appears in the Greek text of Matthew, where Jesus said, "Love your enemies and pray for those who persecute you." It's the word used by Paul, who wrote, "If I speak with the tongues of men and of angels, but have not love, I am become sounding brass, or a clanging cymbal."

Og Mandino helped Floyd understand the meaning of this type of love. It's okay to say to that big, burly, ugly-looking guy, "I love you." It's okay to feel this way about other people.

If you feel this way about other people, then you want to give of yourself in their behalf. This can mean charitable gifts, or it can mean investment of time and talent. At the least, you can give your love unselfishly.

After reading Mandino's book and befriending the lady and her kids, Floyd decided that every week he was going to do something nice for someone that he didn't have to do. He would do it without expecting anything in return.

THE CORPORATE MOTTO

The year Floyd discovered the rewards of giving was also the year he took the Dale Carnegie course. This was a real estate sales class, and the most coveted award was the one for the best sales presentation.

Floyd wanted to win that one—bad. But he didn't make it. Mike Yurek, who was later to work for Floyd, beat him out.

But Floyd won an award that now means more to him than the "best sales presentation" award. It was the award presented to the person who "did the most for the class." It was, in other words, an award for giving.

After he had opened his own company, Floyd decided to make "We Get by Giving" his corporate motto, to be incorporated into the letterhead. In a sense, it had been Floyd's motto for some time. His company had always stressed giving value plus to customers and clients, and when it came to corporate giving, the firm was almost fanatical about giving to everything and everybody.

So when he decided to revise the letterhead, Floyd decided to go even further. He sat down at a table, turned on a tape recorder and poured into it what he called the corporate philosophy. He wanted all employees and trainers to hear it before they started working with the company. He wanted to make sure they fit comfortably into this philosophy. So he explained the "We Get by Giving" concept, and where he had gotten it, including some things he learned from his mother.

The day he recorded that tape was the day Art Fettig's book arrived in the mail.

TITHING 20% OF GROSS

In it, Fettig told about a woman from a wealthy family whom he asked about the secrets of success.

"We tithe," she said.

"Many people tithe," responded Fettig, "yet they are not as talented or as successful as your family."

"We tithe 20%," said the woman.

That's stretching the meaning of "tithe." The word means to give 10%. That's all the Law of Moses required of the Israelites.

But Fettig still wasn't satisfied.

"Surely there is more to that secret," he insisted.

The woman responded: "We tithe 20% of our gross income."[4]

No skimping here. No holding back. No 20% "after taxes and depreciation."

FETTIG'S 'PLATINUM RULE'

Art Fettig gives us his own enhancement of the Golden Rule: "Do unto others as you would have them do unto you, even when you know they are unable to return your generosity and, in fact, obtain a promise from them that under no circumstances will they endeavor to repay you in any way. And do unto others in secret. Then do it even more generously by swearing yourself and the other party to secrecy of your good deed."[5]

Art got his insight from reading Lloyd Douglas' 1929 novel, Magnificent Obsession. He grasped that great novels tell great truths through fictional accounts.

And the great truth told by Magnificent Obsession was no more than our corporate motto: "We Get by Giving."

[4]Art Fettig, The Platinum Rule, (Battle Creek, Michigan: Growth Unlimited Inc., 1988) pp. 46–47.

[5]Ibid, p. 60.

THE $500 RETURN

"Cast thy bread upon the waters," advised the writer of Ecclesiastes, "for thou shalt find it after many days. Give a portion to seven, yea, even unto eight. . . ."

In fact, the Bible is full of stuff about giving generously.

"Freely ye received, freely give," said Jesus himself, and "It is more blessed to give than to receive."

Floyd was in Dallas one day, moments after a successful speaking engagement, when a prosperous-looking young man came up to him and handed him $500 in cash.

It isn't often that somebody hands you $500 right out of the blue. For a moment Floyd thought the guy mistook him for some other kind of salesperson, and was waiting for Floyd to hand him a plastic bag full of white powder.

"What's this for?" Floyd asked.

"It's my repayment," the young man said.

"Repayment for what?"

"Remember several years ago when you were speaking in Denver? You had some cassette albums on sale for $90, I believe. Well, I couldn't afford to pay for them, so I asked you if we could work something out.

"You handed me a whole set of tapes and told me to take them and I could pay for them whenever I was able. You didn't take my name or address or anything.

"Well, I've made good use of those tapes, and I'm happy to say I'm able to pay you back with interest."

This type of thing has happened to me on many occasions. I tell you about it now not to impress you with what a generous guy I am, but to make the point that generosity is one of the secrets to success.

"We Get by Giving" is a motto that applies not just to money.

"You give but little when you give of your possessions," wrote Khalil Gibran in The Prophet. "It is when you give of yourself that you truly give."

If you look up the root meaning of the word "philanthropist," you'll find that it doesn't mean "someone who gives." Rather, it means "lover of mankind." Albert Schweitzer and Mother Theresa were both philanthropists, but they are remembered more for the things *they* did than for the things their money did.

You can express your love for mankind by doing good to your fellow man.

It doesn't have to be something great and noble; you don't have to spend your life in darkest Africa or the slums of India. You can do nice things for all kinds of people—even real estate brokers.

SHARING WITH A COMPETITOR

Not long after Floyd went into real estate management, he was sitting around with several real estate people, showing some of them what he did to get listings.

A broker for another realty firm, a competitor in his market area, said, "You know, Floyd, you should come and do a seminar for me."

He was half joking, and Floyd must have surprised him.

"I'd be happy to share with your people what I do," he told him.

So he did a seminar for the competitor's salespeople. It turned out that the broker also was a good lister. After that, when he'd find that he couldn't get a listing, he would recommend Floyd. Floyd would call the people and get the listing. The two men started trading listings, and both of them benefited.

LESSONS TO LIVE BY

As a street kid on the east side of Detroit; as an aimless swabby in Uncle Sam's Navy, I would never have imagined myself hauling out all the biblical quotes I've used in this part of the book.

I respected the Golden Rule as a general principle, but I never saw it as any kind of guide to prosperity in the business world. The rule on the street, which I might call the "Brass Rule" seemed to have a lot more relevance: "Do it unto others before they do it unto you."

I'm still not a guy who wears his religion on his sleeve. If you cuss in my presence, I won't blush. I don't go around uttering a lot of "Praise the Lords" and "Hallelujahs," though I don't look down on those who do, if that's their way of honoring their God.

But anybody that knows me knows that I live by what I teach. I screw up sometimes in some areas, but I live what I teach, and I swear by the lessons in the Gospels. In fact, I burn with these lessons. They are responsible for my success.

They will carry you to greatness too, if you remember that your giving has to be done unselfishly, with no expectation of reward. Find a person or organization who can use a boost that you can provide. Give that boost. Give it without fanfare and make it clear that you don't expect to be repaid. Give generously to worthy causes at every opportunity. Don't count the cost. Just do it because it's the right thing to do.

A PAUSE TO RECAP

Good teachers pause every so often in their lessons to recap the material they've covered. The teacher in me says it's time to recap. Let's look back at what we've learned.

In Part I of this book, we covered the Four Lessons, which should start you on the **Seven Steps to Achieving Your Full Potential** and provide you with momentum toward greatness. Those four lessons are:

- ❑ **(Lesson 1)** Early choices don't have to bind you for life.
- ❑ **(Lesson 2)** You can't rise to greatness on a bad self-image.
- ❑ **(Lesson 3)** If you don't know what you want, mediocrity is what you'll get.
- ❑ **(Lesson 4)** Greatness won't find you; you have to go after it.

So far, we've covered five of the ***Seven Steps to Achieving Your Full Potential.*** They are:

- ❑ **(Step 1)** Wake up to your capacity for greatness.
- ❑ **(Step 2)** Establish your goals—great ones and small ones.
- ❑ **(Step 3)** Make a commitment.
- ❑ **(Step 4)** Work hard and work smart.
- ❑ **(Step 5)** Give unselfishly in order to get.

Now we're ready for Step Six. Read on.

List the most important points you have gained from the preceding Step:

YOUR FULL POTENTIAL!

Step Six

Give Yourself a Raise

As you keep pursuing your goal of greatness, you'll find that your direction is not always up. You reach plateaus and sometimes it looks as if you'll never be able to climb higher.

When you come to such a situation, it's time to give yourself a raise. You may think you've already hit the ceiling and there's nowhere else to go. How can you give yourself a raise?

There are always higher ceilings. Find them.

About the time I was hanging out on the streets of Detroit learning to move and dress and stare like a cat, a kid who wanted to be a writer was reading the class poem to his graduating class. It concluded with these words:

> There is no top,
> No summit stands alone;
> Nor peak so high
> 'Tis not a steppingstone.

That's a good way of looking at things. Once you tell yourself that you've reached the top, the only way to go is down.

I have another way of looking at it. I think in terms of ceilings instead of peaks. You rise until your head hits the ceiling. Then what do you do? Walk around hunched over at the shoulders so that you don't bump your head?

That's no way to achieve greatness. Walking around hunched over because the ceiling is too low is a good way to get a crick in your back. You're also likely to get claustrophobia. When you've gone as far as you can go in your current job or achievement, either raise it or leave it and find something better.

It's better if you can leave while you're on top. There are several reasons for this. One is obvious: If you leave as a successful person, you're more likely to be invited back, and it's nice to have that option. But the most important reason is that you've got to live with yourself. Nobody wants to leave anywhere as a failure.

That doesn't mean that you should stay in a miserable situation just because you haven't yet advanced to the top. If you're miserable it may be that you're already at your ceiling; you may already have gone as far as you're going in that situation. When you're in that circumstance, you have three choices: Live with it. Leave it. Or change it. It's all in your control, and you can choose.

WHEN THE FOREST IS CLEARED. . . .

Sometimes it's perfectly obvious when you've reached your ceiling.

I'm reminded of the story of the little lumberjack, who stood about 5 feet 4 and weighed about 130 pounds. He walked into a logging camp in Oregon and asked for a job.

The boss looked at him about the way I looked at Dominico Siciliano when he came to me for a job selling real estate.

"You don't look like a lumberjack to me," he said, handing him an axe. "Let me see you chop down that big fir."

The little guy looked at the tree. It was about 90 feet high and six feet across the middle.

The boss man grinned, turned, and began walking back to the stump where he had been sitting.

Before he had taken a dozen steps he heard the little guy yelling, "Timberrrrrrrr!" and the big fir crashed to earth.

The boss man was amazed.

"My God!" he said. "Where did you learn to cut timber like that?"

"In the Sahara," said the little guy.

"But that's a desert."

"It is now," grinned the lumberjack.

The little lumberjack knew when to quit. As soon as he looked around and saw sand dunes instead of trees, it was time to move on to another forest.

At other times it may not be so obvious.

THERE ARE ALWAYS NEW WORLDS

Alexander the Great conquered all the territory from the Mediterranean Sea to the Hindu Kush, and wept because there were no more worlds to conquer. He had reached a ceiling. If he had only known: To the east lay India and China. To the north lay the great expanse of what is now Russia. To the south lay the huge continent of Africa. To the west lay Western Europe and, across the Atlantic, the two great continents of America. Don't make Alexander's mistake: There are always other worlds; other ceilings.

HOW GM BECAME NO. 1

Let me use a Detroit example of someone who did not know when to move on to a new ceiling.

Henry Ford went to the top very quickly in the automobile business. He got there because he built something he didn't really have to go out and sell. All he had to do was to make people aware of it. That "something," of course, was the Model T. It was basic, affordable, reliable transportation for the masses of Americans who could not afford a Buick or Cadillac but nevertheless wanted something a little faster and more convenient than a horse and buggy.

In no time flat, Ford owned the low-priced market. For a while, about 70% of the automobiles sold in this country were Fords. The massive Ford fortune was not made off the Galaxie, or the Thunderbird or the Mustang. It was made off the Model T.

When you own 70% of the market in just about any field, your head is up against the ceiling. It's time to move on.

But Henry Ford didn't want to toy with success. His premise was that the way to stay in the automobile business was to find a design that worked and stick with it. No annual model changes to make the car faster and fancier. No ever-widening choice of colors. You could have any color you wanted so long as it was black.

It worked for a while. Then along came a company called General Motors, which started with Buick, Cadillac, Olds and Oakland as its basic product line and soon added a new make named after an auto-racing enthusiast named Louis Chevrolet.

When it came to producing a new car at the bottom of the American price range, nobody could beat Henry Ford. But the GM executives realized something Ford didn't: After World War I, people didn't have to buy new cars at the bottom of the price range.

Before 1920, most car owners were first-time buyers. If you wanted to buy an automobile, you had little choice but to buy a new one, and you had to come up with the full price for it. During the industry's infancy, used cars were practically non-existent.

But after 1920, buyers had a choice: They could buy a new Model T with no extras at all, or they could buy a used Buick or Olds with a little luxury in the bargain. And a buyer who already owned a Model T and wanted to move up to a nicer car could take the T down to the Olds dealer's and use it for a down payment.

The GM people got smart. They offered a variety of cars, starting with your basic Chevrolet—priced a little higher than the Ford but offering a little more. The buyer could then move up steadily through the Oakland (later the Pontiac), the Oldsmobile, the Buick and finally the Cadillac. GM started making annual model changes, so that this year's model was noticeably different from—and presumably better than—last year's model.

Owners of 1920 Model T's had no incentive to buy new 1922 Model T's because the new cars weren't very different from the old ones. If they wanted something newer or different, they had to trade their Fords in on some other make, and there was the new Chevy—tantalizingly close to the Ford in price but offering just a little more in power, comfort and convenience.

By 1930, Chevrolet had overtaken Ford in the sales race and GM had supplanted Ford as the dominant company in the industry. Ford nearly went bankrupt before Henry II turned the company around following World War II. The reason: When the elder Henry commanded 70% of the market, he didn't realize that his head was at the ceiling and that he needed to move on.

GM found another ceiling and the rest is history.

FROM CEILING TO CEILING

Floyd Wickman has spent his adult life going from one ceiling to another.

The E-5 rating was his ceiling in the Navy. When he realized he wasn't going any higher, he found another ceiling in the real estate field.

After a few years selling real estate, he realized he was at another ceiling. He was surpassing the requirements for the Million Dollar Club regularly. Had there been a Two Million Dollar Club, he would have stuck around longer. Had there been a Forty Million Dollar Club, he might still be selling real estate.

Floyd gave himself a raise by going into sales management. Within a few years, he had the most productive office in his company. He looked for new worlds to conquer, and seeing none in real estate sales, decided to go into sales training.

Had he not been bumping his head against the ceiling, he never would have heard J. Douglas Edwards's call to greatness. He would have heard the words, but they would have sailed over his head because he would have been busy working toward another goal.

But they came at a time when Floyd was looking for another ceiling, and they pointed him toward a new and exciting goal.

Within a few years, he was bumping the ceiling again: He was training director for a nationwide organization. There was nowhere to go within that organization unless he wanted to become the CEO. That chair was already occupied, and the prospect of taking it didn't excite Floyd anyway.

It was time for another raise, so Floyd went looking for another ceiling. He became a professional speaker, determined to be the world's most successful.

The ceiling seemed awfully low and the bumps awfully painful when he went into bankruptcy. But when he looked around he didn't see a desert with no trees. He saw a whole forest waiting to be harvested.

THE GOAL IS THE KEY

The key to finding your way from ceiling to ceiling is having a goal. If you know where you want to go, you will also know whether the path you're on is going to get you there. And there's something about setting goals and making commitments that makes things happen for you.

Floyd has been asked about the source of his creativity. He doesn't spend a lot of time trying to pinpoint where it comes from. He knows that for the first 26 years of his life he hardly had a creative thought. But once he became aware of his potential, set his goals and made his commitments, the creativity emerged.

He doesn't think the creativity comes out of thin air. Rather, it emerges from the mass of experiences—negative and positive—that Floyd has accumulated over the years. It's the commitment to a goal that calls these experiences to the surface.

One of the more successful programs the Wickman company has offered in recent years is "Rapid Fire Recruiting," a course for management. It's a creative approach to recruiting personnel and it's based on Floyd's own experiences. It's not something that came to him in a daydream, and he darn sure didn't pick it up at Harvard Business School.

BECOMING THE HEAD HOG

In fact, if you're looking for someone with a string of degrees and honorary titles, don't come looking for Floyd Wickman. If you want to introduce him by title, just call him the Head Hog.

In the world of sales, that will immediately ring a bell, because at this writing, the Floyd Wickman Course—Sweathogs® is the nation's number-one results-oriented real estate sales course.

He started it in 1980, and it has changed the lives of tens of thousands of participants. Sweathogs®, on average, graduate from the program and increase their productivity by 250%.

The term "Sweathog" is not original with Floyd, as every follower of prime-time television knows. It was introduced via the television series "Welcome Back Kotter," Kotter being a teacher assigned to a class of underdogs.

"Sweathogs" was what they called those kids who had to work extra hard to gain the respect and recognition of others in the school.

Floyd developed a 12-week course designed to take low to average achievers in the sales world and turn them into prosperous, productive professionals.

One night he joked to the participants that he felt like Mr. Kotter working with the hard core.

"I guess that makes us Sweathogs," said one of the group.

And the name stuck.

NEEDED: MORE HOGS

In time Floyd was up against a ceiling again. There are only 365 days a year and there's only one Floyd Wickman. No matter how good he was at teaching this course, he could teach only so many a year.

So he got out from under that ceiling by training others to follow his instructional techniques. At this writing, he has 44 trainers nationwide and an administrative staff of 15.

Floyd packs into this course all the practical techniques for sales success that he learned during his years in the real estate business. He teaches them all the basics—laying foundations, working smart to save time, making the most of appointments, separating lookers from buyers, putting the telephone to work and closing sales.

But the program involves more than just information. It builds up an esprit de corps that is often characteristic of people who go through a tough experience and emerge better for it. One graduate told Floyd that 70% of his referrals were coming from fellow Sweathogs®.

IT'S NO CAKE WALK

The Floyd Wickman Course—Sweathogs® is a tough experience. It's no cake walk, but then people who walk around in circles don't list or sell many properties.

Floyd and his trainers lay down the rules: You come to class on time. You don't miss classes. You complete your assignments. A missed class counts for a strike. So do other infractions. Three strikes and you're out of the course, with no refunds. The Floyd Wickman of the '50s would have flunked out in less time that it took to hot-wire a '56 Mercury.

"It looks like boot camp," said Calvin Ladd of Calhoun Realty in Edina, Minnesota.

In fact, there's a Sweathogs® uniform—an orange team tee shirt—just to give people a sense of belonging.

But it isn't all grunting and sweating. Every meeting opens and closes with a song, and the instructors serve up a mixture of tough tasks, motivational challenges and fun.

The program consists of four-hour sessions one day a week. The rest of the week, the Sweathogs® are expected to put the lessons into practice.

But before they try the techniques on actual prospects, they practice on each other. After they've taken them into the field, they return the next week to report on the results.

"There's nothing better than grabbing hold of a great idea and running with it," said A. J. Harrison of Century 21-Emery in Huntington Beach, California. "Sweathogs® is set up to let you do just that. One day a week you attend the actual session, load up on great selling strategies and get fired up. The rest of the week you're free to apply those strategies on the job. The immediate reinforcement is invaluable. I produced over $7 million in volume in 12 weeks."

Gosh, A. J., in California that must have meant selling two whole houses!

But in Milliken, Ontario, it isn't so easy. Steven Chen of South Breeze Realty there reported selling or listing 104 units during the 12-week course.

"Today my volume is $3.5 million," he said. "That's flying."

The Floyd Wickman Course—Sweathogs® has been referred to a number of times, and for good reason. Whatever the future of the course, it has produced dramatic results. These results aren't all attributable to sales skills learned. Much of the program is devoted to teaching the principles dealt within this book.

The nice thing about all this is that it dovetails perfectly with the corporate motto: "We get by giving." Floyd gives them the benefit of all the knowledge he's picked up through the school of hard knocks. They pay him a fair price for his services. The exchange is making them and him rich.

One person who is familiar with Floyd's work has referred to him as "the Levi's of the speaking business."

"He's not real smooth, but his material is durable," he said.

Floyd took that as a compliment.

ANOTHER CEILING?

Floyd's goal was to be the world's number-one real estate speaker. He's closed in on that. Floyd's goal is to become the world's number-one sales speaker. He's closing on that. Whatever your gauge, he's been moving toward that goal: in the number of speeches he gives; in the number of return engagements; in the number of people who hear him; in the fees he commands for each talk.

Floyd has keynoted every major convention in the real estate industry. He has spoken in every state and from coast to coast in Canada.

The National Speakers Association, with its 2,500 members, bestowed upon him its Council of Peers Award of Excellence, which he shares with such luminaries as Ronald Reagan, Art Linkletter, Norman Vincent Peale, Tom Winninger, Tom Hopkins and one of his idols, Zig Ziglar. Fewer than 80 people have been awarded this honor since the beginning of NSA.

So where does he go from here?

You can bet he won't be like Henry Ford the elder, staying under that same ceiling while some General Motors of professional speaking steals the market out from under him.

Maybe he'll write the all-time best-selling book on how to become a success, regardless of your start in life.

Yeah. Maybe he'll call it, The Wickman Formula: The Seven Steps to Achieving Your Full Potential.

List the most important points you have gained from the preceding Step:

YOUR FULL POTENTIAL!

Step Seven

Practice the 'Dance of Greatness'

The last of the **Seven Steps to Achieving Your Full Potential** is really a dance. It's one you'll find yourself doing involuntarily, for the most part. Most people have to dance their way to greatness because, usually, the path is not a straight, level run from Point A to Point B. It's a progression of steps in a slow dance. You go forward three steps, then back two. Sometimes you go back two before you advance three.

Why is this true?

Because every life and every career has its ups and downs. Regardless of what you undertake, you're likely to fail at first until you develop the right skills, uncover the right formula, or come across the right line of endeavor.

Don't let that discourage you. Henry Ford didn't invent the Model T the first time he tinkered with a gasoline engine. Albert Einstein didn't hit upon the Theory of Relativity the first time he sat down to figure out the universe. Who knows? Fred Astaire may have stepped on Ginger Rogers' toes a few times before he achieved greatness as a dancer.

Life is a learning process, and we learn from our failures.

At least that's how it has always been with Floyd Wickman. If he had given up when the direction of progress changed, he would have swabbed decks in the Navy for 20 years, then retired. Who knows? By now he might be living in a mobile home in Florida, swatting mosquitoes and looking over his shoulder for alligators.

Floyd's glad he danced through to the finish. He likes Michigan winters, he hates mosquitoes, and he never saw an alligator he'd care to turn his back on.

Those who don't expect to take a few steps backward should stay off the dance floor.

Let's trace Floyd's dance steps down through the years:

Up three: *He was a good kid, never got into trouble, and learned to be a hard, meticulous worker while making the rounds with his dad on the milk route.*

Back two: *Then he fell in with a street gang, swiped cars, flunked two grades in school, got sent to a detention home and quit school in the ninth grade.*

Up three: *He joined the Navy and found steady employment.*

Back two: *He flunked the scholastic phase of boot camp.*

Up three: *His good work habits enabled him to become the storekeeper for a Navy cruiser—a job that usually goes to a senior enlisted man.*

Back two: *His bad attitude got him nowhere so far as advancement through the ranks.*

Up three: *He left the Navy and invested in a milk route.*

Back two: *Between the hoodlums that robbed him and the people who moved away without paying, he was going broke.*

Up three: *He met and married Linda and accepted the Navy's offer to return to the ranks and train reservists in his hometown of Detroit.*

Back two: *He flunked the aptitude test for a Navy trainer.*

Up three: *The Navy took him anyway, and he landed a job running the Navy Exchange.*

Back two: *His bad attitude reasserted itself, he goofed off, got busted in rank, and went back to civilian life. His lack of purpose and direction also got his marriage off to a rocky start.*

Up three: *He landed a job selling real estate for the company where his brother-in-law worked.*

Back two: *He bombed during his first 11 months in real estate, getting few listings, making few sales, and getting broker by the minute.*

Up three: *After a brief try at selling insurance, he returned to real estate and began working for a tyrant he called Hitler's Brother. H.B. refused to put up with Floyd's sloppy work habits, pointed him toward a sales-training course and said, "Take it." Floyd took it, began making the Million Dollar Club year after year, and soon entered sales management. He made a commitment to his family as well as to his career, and his marriage blossomed.*

Back two: *He gave up his lucrative sales and management career to become a sales trainer at $1,000 a month.*

Up three: *After a year of hard work and learning, he was offered* *a job as regional trainer for a nationwide real estate company. Eventually he became the company's national training director.*

Back two: *Then he gave up his security and good pay to strike out on his own as a professional speaker.*

Up three: *He had two good years as a public speaker, grossing upwards of $250,000 a year.*

Back two: *In his third year, he went into Chapter 11 bankruptcy.*

Up three: *He got up off the floor and launched some innovative programs in sales training.*

He's still into that last step, moving toward his goal of becoming the world's top sales speaker.

Think about your own life and the things you've accomplished. I'll bet that many of your successes came after failures, and that in some ways you've been "dancing" your whole life.

PROGRESS IS NOT AUTOMATIC

The dance steps don't come automatically—especially the three steps forward. A lot of hard work is involved.

Another important thing to understand is this: The backward steps are not all negatives. If we take the trouble to learn from our mistakes during the two steps backward, we set the stage for those three steps forward.

You'll also notice that some of the backward steps were taken deliberately. Sometimes it's necessary to step backward before we can take the three steps forward.

Floyd gave up a hefty annual income to become vice president in charge of recruiting and training for Lee Real Estate. A grand a month was not a princely salary, even in the middle '70s. But he turned that year into a whirlwind experience and stored up a lot of credits to be cashed in during years to come.

He interviewed 800 people for real estate jobs that year. He also got a chance to design programs and practice his speaking and training techniques. He would need that experience when he began to design training programs on his own. And when he began to market his services as a speaker with expertise in sales training, it was helpful to have all those people out there in real estate who knew him and had been recruited and trained by him.

All these assets were out there to be tapped once Floyd had completed his two steps backward and was ready for his three steps forward.

Then came that breakfast with Zig Ziglar, the concept of "Ask and ye shall receive," and the invitation to join Realty World. A year after he had entered the sales-training field, he became a regional trainer for a nationwide firm, responsible now for 80 offices, not just seven.

THE DANCE CONTINUES

The dance continued when Floyd reached out for the position of national training director for Realty World. He went in to interview for the job, and he thought it went pretty well. But he didn't get it. Two steps back.

It wasn't that the people in top management didn't love him. They just loved somebody else better. But the somebody else wasn't totally committed to Realty World, and before long he left the organization.

That's when the word went out: "Send for Floyd." Three steps forward. Floyd wasn't proud. Second choice or not, he took the job. He now was in charge of training for a company with hundreds of offices nationwide.

The new job meant moving from Detroit to the Virginia suburbs of Washington, D.C. Linda wasn't ecstatic over the move, but she was supportive.

And Floyd went at it with the kind of commitment that had been his trade mark since his moment of truth during the STI course.

He redesigned all the Realty World manuals. He trained or retrained their trainers.

But he didn't forget his goal: to address that audience of 2,300 by April 16, 1979. The Realty World experience was a means toward that goal. Floyd achieved it, then decided to go into business on his own as a professional speaker.

He went from a secure job with a solid, substantial firm to a job with no security except for his own confidence and ability.

FLOYD WHO?

Floyd had enough money to rent a U-Haul truck. He put Linda and the two younger boys—Gino and David—on a plane for Detroit. Floyd and Floyd Jr. drove that U-Haul through a blizzard from Washington to Detroit. He borrowed money for a house from a real estate agent, and had $3,130 left over. On that shoestring, he started his present business.

The whole country was suffering from a bad case of "Floyd Who?" and Floyd wasn't sure how long his family could eat on $3,130.

But the dance pattern held true. During his years of recruiting and training for other people, he had built up a certain amount *of brand equity. He capitalized on that, and in his first year as a professional speaker he grossed $260,000.*

In the second year he did better than that. In the third year came the Chapter 11 bankruptcy. Two big steps backward.

How did it happen?

Well, the basic explanation for any bankruptcy is that your expenses are more than your income. If you want to go deeper than that, I'll make this observation: I was on the road most of the time and lost touch with the organization. I had not taken the trouble to communicate my basic philosophy to the people who worked for me. They did not set goals, and so therefore they did not make commitments. And the people working with me were not givers. I can't put it any simpler than that.

On a nuts and bolts level, the speaking business was still doing fine, but the organization allowed itself to get into the ticket-selling business. The staff would sell tickets for a one-day seminar or a three-day seminar. I learned a great lesson then: If you've got a product or service that you have to go out and sell to people, you've got the wrong product or service. You need a product or a service that people will want once they become aware of it.

At that time, we were offering people a very orthodox program: a six-hour seminar on listing and selling techniques; a three-day seminar on closing techniques. There was nothing unique about the program.

MILLSTONE OR ROCKET?

The bankruptcy taught Floyd something: Adversity can be either a millstone around your neck or a booster rocket to greater things.

Floyd turned his into a booster rocket. He took stock of where the problems lay, brought his business into line with his *philosophies, and in his fourth year as a professional speaker brought in $1.2 million.*

From then on, it has been up, up, up all the way, the net following the gross. Floyd now runs the third largest sales-training business in the world, and the top one in the real estate business. The company has expanded beyond the real estate field and into the automotive and financial-planning industries.

KEEP MOVING

As you progress toward greatness, you're going to encounter setbacks. Don't let them discourage you. Regard each setback as a valuable lesson. Look for the reasons behind the failure. Did you lose sight of your goal? Did you go in without the proper commitment? Did you fail to make an adequate investment?

Or were you simply premature, tackling a major challenge before you had acquired the necessary education and training.

Decide what you need to do to make a success the next time around. Then go back in, determined that you're not going to repeat your mistakes. If you fail again, fall back and analyze once again the source of your failure. If you accept each failure as a positive learning experience, you'll eventually find the formula for greatness, and you can break into the dance of joy.

When you've achieved your goal of greatness, look around you. You're not on top of a lofty peak. You're bumping against another ceiling. Look for new worlds to conquer.

There are other opportunities for greatness all around you. Become aware of them. Set yourself a new and loftier goal. Make a commitment to that goal. Work hard and work smart to achieve it. Give generously of your time, talent and resources to help others achieve greatness. When your head seems to be striking a ceiling, look for a higher ceiling. Continue in the Dance of Greatness. Remember that there will be times when you'll have to take some steps backward. But as soon as you start stepping back, begin to look around for the direction of your next forward movement.

Successful people don't stand still. They move. Sometimes they move forward and sometimes they move backwards. The secret of the dance of success is to make your steps forward outnumber your steps backward.

List the most important points you have gained from the preceding Step:

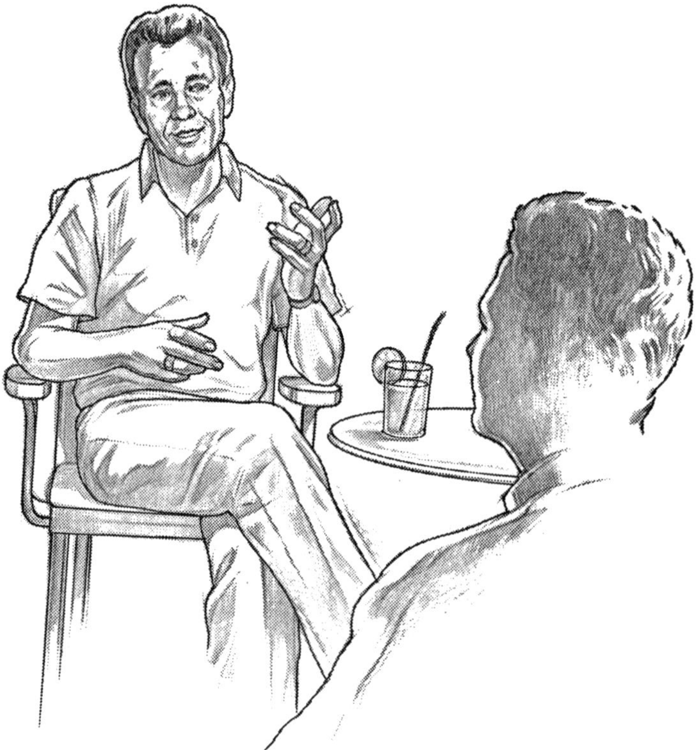

One on One With Floyd Wickman

There's nothing I enjoy more than helping a person solve a problem. Let's pretend we're best friends, sitting on your porch sipping lemonade, and you have some burning personal questions you want to ask me. And you know I won't beat around the bush—I'll be straightline with you. Because I'm your best friend.

I have 25 years in this people business, and believe me when I say I know why some people succeed and why some people fail. What I have seen in my 25 years in this business is that there are common problems in any industry, and I have come out with what I call, for lack of a better term, "philosophies" that not only answer those common problems, but also help you see how much simpler your life and successes could be.

I chose to dedicate this section of my book to those philosophies in hope that when it's all said and done, after you've read this book, these philosophies become a part of you. I hope these philosophies will give you answers to your problems, and give you inspiration whenever you need it.

Let's talk. . . .

YOU: Floyd, I'm in an environment I am not happy in. What should I do? What are my choices?

FLOYD: **If you don't like your environment, you have three choices: Live with it. Leave it. Or change it.** Which one of these choices do you have the most control over? And which one of these would please you the most? What's your decision?

YOU: I don't know my decision. It's the indecision that hurts.

FLOYD: Anytime in our lives when we are in a state of indecision about something we care about, we go into an emotional holding pattern. We then become useless to our jobs, our families, and to ourselves. **It's less important what you decide than it is that you decide.** The minute you make a decision, you come out of this emotional holding pattern. The choices are not what's stopping you; it's the fact that you're procrastinating in making this decision.

YOU: Floyd, how come some people are born with silver spoons in their mouths? How did these people get to be so special?

FLOYD: **There's nothing special about special people; it's what they do that makes them special, not "who" they are.** Everyone has the same doubts and insecurities as anyone else. "Special people" rise to greatness by the activities they take up during their years. Pedigree or personality doesn't have a bearing on becoming "special" or "great." It's what you do every day that will make you special.

YOU: Well, if these special people are normal people just like you and me, what is their rule of thumb? How do they know what to do, and when to do it?

FLOYD: Look at your present and past and figure out what you have always enjoyed doing, and do well. Take what you do well, channel that toward accomplishment, and stick to it, never giving up. Look at what you want (your goal) as a process. Take that smallest step first, and work on completing that. **You have to take it one step at a time, and stay on track.** You can't worry about the end result now. If you do what makes you happy and you're rewarded in some way for your efforts, your journey to greatness will be a lot more fun.

YOU: How do I get the energy to go on this journey? To take all these steps? Floyd, I have such a long way to go.

FLOYD: In your life and in my life, when we are working toward a specific, attainable, visualized, written-down goal, we are at the highest degree of energy. When you do feel apathetic or have the least amount of energy is when you are not working toward a goal. Goals give you physical energy.

YOU: Floyd, I have so much adversity in my past. In many ways, more than you have had. How am I supposed to react when these bad things hit me in the face and send me flying backwards?

FLOYD: Always remember this: No matter who we are—how "special" we are—we all have adversities. Think of the old saying: "If you think you've got it bad, go visit a hospital." The question is: Are you going to look at your **adversities as an anchor or a booster rocket?** If you want to make them booster rockets, you have to learn from them, let them go, and go on with your life. You have no other alternative except to allow them to be anchors—and let them drown you.

YOU: Floyd, what can I possibly do when the market conditions and economy are bad and it affects my job?

FLOYD: **When the going gets tough, the tough get back to the basics.** Every industry has "basics." Remember what you did when you first started in the first week of your job? How about the first month? Those "basic" things that helped you get started and got you to the level you are at now. Maybe your superstar salesman colleague makes his whole business from referrals. But not too long ago, he had to pick up the phone and call strangers from a phone book. Or knock on plenty of doors. Every business has the basics. Say it's a retail store. What got you to a certain level was that first grand opening, and that special service given to all the customers by the smiling employees. Well, if the economy gets bad, have another grand opening, and have your employees give it their all in customer service.

YOU: Floyd, some people in my life are not supportive of the goals and aspirations that I want to accomplish some day. What can I do about these people?

FLOYD: **You are responsible <u>to</u> other people, but not <u>for</u> them.** In other words, you are responsible to deliver what you promise to people, to be the best person you can be. But you are not responsible for their reactions. Ask yourself who you really are responsible to. Associate yourself with people who are "encouragers." They'll help you to the road of greatness; the "discouragers" will keep you in mediocrity.

YOU: Floyd, I feel that I'm constantly seeking the approval of others, and trying to please everyone except myself. I usually feel dissatisfied with myself for doing this.

FLOYD: If you're doing things for other people's approval, more times than not, you're going to be let down. **Do the things that make you feel good, because more times than not, waiting for others to praise you will lead to disappointment.**

YOU: Floyd, sometimes I feel that my personality gets in the way of my job or in social settings. How can I change my personality?

FLOYD: Sorry. You might not like my answer. Accept who you are. Don't try to change your personality. It's virtually impossible. **Personality is not what takes you to greatness. Your characteristics will take you to greatness.** If you're going to change anything about **you,** change some of your characteristics. Are you always late? Change to being punctual. Are you loyal and trustworthy? Be that person whose word is respected. Work on your characteristics. Because if you develop strong, respectful characteristics, they will overshadow any personality flaws that you may have.

YOU: How can I work so hard to attain my goals and still have time for my family and friends?

FLOYD: First, learn to separate your professional from your personal life. **People who don't separate their professional from their personal lives eventually pay a high price.** It isn't the quantity of time that you spend on something; it's the quality of the time. You can't give 10 hours to your job, 10 hours to your family, and two hours to clean house, run errands, take a shower and do your banking. With the other two hours visiting your grandmother. When would you sleep or eat? You can't burn the candle at both ends. But you can be super-productive at your job for, say, nine hours and spend three or four quality hours with your family. Take the necessary steps to reach your goals. But don't let it diminish the commitments or responsibilities you have with other people. Yes, quality is much more important than the quantity of time. Even if you spend only four hours at work one day. It could be the most productive, quality four hours you have ever spent at your company.

YOU: Floyd, I deal with people every day and I give them the best service I can. I know my product. I work hard. I give exciting presentations. But I can't seem to get people to buy from me. What am I doing wrong? Is sales for me?

FLOYD: Yes, sales is for you. However, you are missing one important ingredient to the sales process. **People don't care what you know until they know that you care.** Spend more time polishing those interpersonal skills to show people that you do indeed care, and are interested in their problems. Dr. Elliot Wagenheim once taught me this: Caring about what others care about is what caring about is all about. In other words, if you show people that you care about what's important to them, you're going to draw them to you like a magnet. The best example I can give you is my son and his motorcycle. I'm a father, and I hate motorcycles because they are so dangerous. But when I finally learned this truth about "caring," I went out and bought my son a motorcycle helmet for Christmas. You know, since then, we have been closer to each other than we have ever been?

YOU: What is the secret of "selling" to people?

FLOYD: **If you have a product that you feel you really have to "sell" to people, you're selling the wrong product.** But if you have a product that people want when they become aware of it, then you're selling the right product. If you are doing everything right, including letting the client know that you care, you must be selling the wrong product.

YOU: What is the secret in obtaining my financial security?

FLOYD: **No investment is too small to begin with, because great wealth doesn't come from big investments.** It comes from small investments that are steppingstones to a continuance of investments. Tuck that $100 away somewhere and promise yourself you won't touch it for a year. At the end of that year, I'll guarantee you won't touch it. Why? Because now you have something, as opposed to nothing. Your $100 perhaps has earned interest, and it's even more precious to you. You see, **it is what you do when you don't have to that determines what you're going to be when you can no longer help it.**

YOU: I've been working hard for so many years to reach a certain income level. I still haven't reached it. What am I doing wrong?

FLOYD: **If you spend your life chasing money, it will never catch you.** The trick is to do what you do for the personal satisfaction, the praise, the awards, the fame, or whatever. And if it's a capitalistic venture, the money will come to you automatically. Working for the money is like trying to make someone love you: The harder you try, the further you'll push them away. As soon as you sit back, relax, and allow yourself to be yourself, love will come. Remember: If money is your sole motivation, eventually you'll be forced to cheat. And that cheating may destroy everything you've built for yourself.

YOU: Floyd, what is the single most important factor in determining how people end up—either in mediocrity or in greatness?

FLOYD: If you think I'm successful and you're concerned that you're not, remember: **The only difference between you and me is that you believed you were going to fail, and I believed I was going to succeed.** I know of so many people who go to success seminars, read self help books, and are always, always working on how to be successful. They can't figure out why they are not successful when they're getting all the help and advice they could ever ask for. Still, what's missing? They don't believe that they can be successful. I highly recommend the book by James Allen, As a Man Thinketh. Read it 10 times. You'll see the light.

PHILOSOPHIES TO LIVE YOUR LIFE BY TO ACHIEVE YOUR FULL POTENTIAL

Take these philosophies to heart. Write them down on a personal sheet of paper. Repeat them to yourself 10 times every day for the next 30 days. These philosophies are not simple adages or proverbs. They are as real and true as I am. Believe in these. Trust in them. It took me a total of 49 years to accumulate and understand this wisdom, which may sound very simple or basic to you. But it works. If your last question to me were, "What is the secret to your success, Floyd?" I would answer with these philosophies.

1. If you don't like your environment, you have three choices: Live with it, leave it, or change it

2. It's less important what you decide than it is that you decide.

3. There's nothing special about "special" people; it's what they do that makes them special, not "who" they are.

4. Take it one step at a time, and always stay on track.

5. Set a goal, and you'll get the physical energy you've been lacking.

6. Adversities can be an anchor or a booster rocket—it's up to you.

7. When the going gets tough, the tough get back to the basics.

8. You are responsible **to** other people, but not **for** them.

9. Associate yourself with people who are "encouragers." They'll help you to the road of greatness; the "discouragers will keep you in mediocrity.

10. Do the things that make you feel good because, more times than not, waiting for others to praise you will lead to disappointment.

11. **Personality** is not what takes you to greatness; your **characteristics** will take you to greatness.

12. People who don't separate their professional lives from their personal lives eventually pay a high price.

13. People don't **care what you know** until they **know that you care.**

14. Caring about what others care about is what caring about is all about.

15. If you have a product that you feel you really have to **sell** to people, you're selling the wrong product.

16. No investment is too small to begin with, because great wealth doesn't always come from big investments.

17. It is what you do when you don't have to that determines what you're going to be when you can no longer help it.

18. The only difference between someone successful and you, if you consider yourself unsuccessful, is that you believed you were going to fail and the other chose to believe he was going to succeed.

Epilogue

Somewhere in the preceding pages, I hope you've found the key that unlocks the door to success for you.

There's been a lot of Floyd Wickman in this book, because the lessons I've learned have all come from the life of Floyd Wickman as it has been touched by others.

I'm a happy man today and am still working toward accomplishing much more because I have put those lessons into practice. The happiness comes not just from my own success. You haven't known true fulfillment until you have seen people who have been wallowing in failure or low achievement suddenly soar to success on the wings of your help and advice.

I've had that pleasure, and if this book is an instrument that helps you spread your wings, my pleasure will be greatly enhanced.

As a ninth-grade dropout, I don't have any scholarly pretensions. But I sometimes find that those who have taken the academic path come up with conclusions very similar to those I reached while taking the thorny path of experience.

Much of what I have been telling you is summed up in the

"Five L's" of Dr. Barrie Greiff, a psychiatrist who taught at Harvard Business School.

Greiff says that to succeed you have to develop the ability to learn, to labor, to love, to laugh and to leave.

We covered the learning part when we talked about awareness: waking up to the possibilities within oneself and taking the steps to realize those possibilities.

After the awareness comes the goal-setting. Setting a goal paves the way for further learning, because it naturally focuses the mind on acquiring the basic information and skills needed to reach the goal.

Then comes commitment—a determination to reach the goal and to make the necessary investment in time and resources.

This takes us to the second "L"—labor. Hard work is required, but it can also be rewarding work.

Add to your labor the ingredient of love, as embodied in the Golden Rule and Art Fettig's "Platinum Rule." Give unselfishly of your time and resources to provide for others that extra boost they need to proceed under their own steam.

The fourth "L" is laughter. I've tried to sprinkle this book with a few dashes of humor to make the learning easier and the reading more enjoyable. I do the same thing in my speeches and training seminars. The Floyd Wickman Course—Sweathogs®, for instance, calls for a lot of hard work, but we do a lot of laughing too.

The fifth "L," the ability to leave, may seem a strange ingredient in the recipe for success.

But Greiff's formula only confirms the experience of my life: There comes a time when your head is bumping against the ceiling. When that moment arrives, it's time to get ready to leave; time to look around for a higher ceiling.

How long should you keep looking for higher ceilings?

For as long as there's something above the ceiling you're working under.

Epilogue

THE OLD MAN, THE BOYS AND THE BIRD

Will these lessons and seven steps work for you? The answer is in your hands. I'd like to illustrate my point by telling you a story. It's a fable. It happened long, long ago, in a land far, far, far away. At the foot of a large mountain existed a tiny village. In the village lived two mischievous boys. At the top of the mountain lived an old man, reputed to be the wisest man on Earth. One day, the two boys came up with an idea that, they thought, would make them famous. Their idea was to pose a question to the old, wise man; a question that he couldn't possibly answer. Then they would achieve glorious fame! Their idea was to capture a small bird, hold it tightly in their hands, and ask the old man if the bird was dead or alive. If the old man said the bird was alive, they'd simply crush their hands together. If the old man said the bird was dead, they'd open their hands and let the bird fly out. Either way, the old wise man would be wrong, and the boys would be famous! The day finally came. The boys climbed to the top of the mountain with the small bird. In nervous anticipation, the boys asked the old man the question.

"In our hands is a bird. Is the bird dead or alive?" To which the old man responded instantly, "The answer is in your hands."

Let's repeat my question. Will these lessons and seven steps work for you? I can only respond: The answer is in ***your*** hands.

For Further Information

For information on Floyd Wickman's availability to speak at your next seminar, rally, or convention, or for questions regarding this book or other Floyd Wickman products, write Floyd Wickman Associates, 1707 West Big Beaver Road, Troy, Michigan 48084 or call 1-800-548-7733.